Beyond Mere Motherhood

BEYOND
Mere Motherhood

Moms Are People Too

Cindy Rollins

BLUE SKY
DAISIES

Wichita, Kansas

Beyond Mere Motherhood: Moms Are People Too
© *Cindy Rollins 2023*

Published by Blue Sky Daisies
blueskydaisies.net
Wichita, Kansas

Cover and interior images (floral pattern and bird): olga.korneeva via Creative Market

Website URLs referenced in these pages were current at the time of publication but may change over time.

Cover Design Blue Sky Daisies © 2023

ISBN: 978-1-944435-41-7

Contents

Foreword

The Habit of Being a Mother

I was a homeschooling mother. This is somewhat like being a teenage werewolf. It is weird. While I wrote this book based on my own experiences of motherhood, which included homeschooling, I hope the scope of the book is helpful to all mothers and daughters. Many homeschooling mothers work outside their homes or have paying gigs at home. I wrote this for all of you. This is not some sort of how-to-be-a-homemaker book, although I hope it will help you make your home beautiful from the inside out. This is a book about the women I know and the things they face and feel. Some have jobs and some don't. Elisabeth Elliot encouraged women to find Titus 2 mentors, and even worse, she encouraged women to be Titus 2 mentors. Most older women I know feel too inadequate for that title. That is why I wrote this book—to illustrate that they are not.

Cindy Rollins
2023

Introduction

This is a book about self-education. It is not a book about homeschooling our children so much as about homeschooling ourselves. In that way, it is not a book for homeschooling moms only but for all moms who want to become educated in the midst of a busy life.

It is not a book about parenting. It is a book about how a mother can capture her moments and days in such a way that they add up to a life worth living. Her life.

I hope as you are reading this book the lines between spirit, body, and mind become blurred, seamless. Our minds, bodies, and spirits are a trivium, a trinity, best kept in balance. In point eighteen of her twenty principles, Charlotte Mason says:

> We should allow no separation to grow up between the intellectual and "spiritual" life of children; but should teach them that the divine Spirit has constant access to their spirits, and is their continual helper in all the interests, duties and joys of life.

We should allow no separation to grow in our own adult lives either.

1

A. W. Tozer, in his book *The Pursuit of God*, caps off a masterful work with a masterful chapter on the importance of not separating the sacred from the secular. This does not mean that we have to over-spiritualize our pursuits to make them acceptable. You know how we tack spiritual things on to secular things to make them seem noble? Like singing a hymn while changing the baby's diaper or making sure we read a Bible verse at book club? It means that our regular, ordinary, daily tasks are already spiritual. Maybe we just feel like singing hymns while changing the diaper or maybe not. Either way the diaper changing is sacred and so is the hymn, if our hearts are tuned towards our Creator.

CHAPTER ONE

The Thinking Mother

> Let us practice the fine art of making every work a
> priestly ministration. Let us believe that God is in all
> our simple deeds and learn to find Him there.
>
> A. W. Tozer, *The Pursuit of God*

Ordo Amoris

I used to think that I had been cheated out of an education by
the system. After graduating from high school woefully ignorant,
I began my own course of self-education. This has been both gratifying and frustrating as I discovered for myself that the more you
know the more there is to know. One thing I know now is that
all education is ultimately self-education. I hadn't been cheated by
the system; the system itself was never able to perform the task. It
had always been up to me, just as your education has always been
up to you. Over the years, I have noticed people from different elementary and high school educational venues complaining about
the education they received. Just like I did.

I grew up in Florida public schools. A friend who attended private Christian schools all her life would never send her children to
one of those. And many grown-up homeschoolers complain about
the poor education they got from their mothers. I have begun to
look at all these complaints kind of like those pesky internet ads.
They don't reflect the site you are visiting so much as you. We all

wake up one day, no matter what school we attended, and realize that there is a lot out there that we do not know. If we don't have that awakening, then we are ignorant indeed. We can look backwards and blame this lack on the schools we attended, or we can look forward and try to remedy the problem, recognizing that education belongs to the individual. As a homeschooling mom, I am not entirely sure I educated my children well; they weren't always paying attention, but I do know that I was paying attention, and I was being educated while trying to teach them. In that way, you could almost say that I had been saved by bearing children. (I Timothy 2:15 says, "Yet she will be saved through childbearing— if they continue in faith and love and holiness, with self-control.") Teaching my own children taught me how to learn, how to see, how to pay attention.

The truth is that all humans are always seeing something, paying attention to something, learning something. Perhaps, we are learning every sort of sexual innuendo known to man by watching endless reruns of *Friends*. Perhaps, we are learning how to fit in socially and politically by spending hours and hours on social media. Perhaps we are paying attention, day and night, to what we don't have, wasting our time on Earth in envy, frustration, and discontent. We are paying attention to something. Maybe it isn't verb tenses, or the periodic table of elements, or the Great Books, but we are all being educated by our loves. Recognizing that maybe what we love is unworthy is the first step in being truly educated. What is worthy of this love I have? What is worthy of my time and attention? Let me tell you a secret. Education is free. It is simply a matter of opening your eyes and acknowledging the "I don't know."

I noticed, at first accidentally and later by paying attention, that even people with elite college degrees are missing much of what previous generations believed made up the educated human. I recently was talking to a seminarian with a doctorate who had never heard of *Hamlet*. This is not an isolated incidence. We have become so focused on that sheepskin that we failed to notice that it was not what we thought it was. In our culture, people cling to their degrees to justify their very existence, yet all the while they have been cheated out of knowledge. Most of them never even know what they have lost. Clinging to their "diploma" has left them as dull and ignorant as the pilgrim named Ignorance in *Pilgrim's Progress* who wanted to get into the Kingdom without his certificate. These people think their certificate is a free pass.

> It is time to wake up and meet the creation. It was made just for you.

It has been said that we are what we behold. The Bible says that we see through a glass darkly, but someday we shall see face to face. Someday, if we know Christ, we will see, and therefore know, all things because we will see and know the One who created it all. The pursuit of knowledge (the creation) is ultimately the pursuit of the knowledge of God (the Creator). Sure you are ignorant. Sure you were cheated. You have been cheating yourself by paying attention to the wrong things. But the good news is that now is the day of salvation. All is not lost. It is time to wake up and meet the creation. It was made just for you.

What are your loves?

Maybe it is time to reorder them. Maybe when you consider where you spend your time, you will be surprised to find your loves are not what you think they are nor what you would like them to be. Ouch. That is not at all unusual. We like to think of ourselves in a certain light, but what we spend our time on tells a different tale.

Now is the time to ask yourself the hard questions. Sometimes we don't notice that the seasons of our life have changed. Maybe we had morning sickness and spent three months lounging on the couch too sick to even watch YouTube. Maybe we didn't notice that we were feeling better until we started binge-watching Hallmark movies. This is completely understandable (sort of). When things feel out of control, we gravitate to perfect fantasy worlds. Seasons change frequently in the life of a mother, sometimes suddenly. We didn't notice that the baby stopped nursing, or that the seven-year-old got potty-trained. All that time spent sitting on the edge of the bathtub handing out marshmallows is now free time. All that time singing "John Jacob Jingleheimier Schmidt" and "Where is Thumbkin?" is inexplicably free, at least for now. Some seasons are welcome and some are scary, but whenever the seasons of a mother's life change, it is good to be aware that opportunities to read and grow also change. There will come a day when much of your reading will be done on the go. When our son Christopher got blood poisoning from a spider bite, I made sure to remind him to bring a book to the emergency room. I looked up to see he was reading *The Grim Reaper* by Piet Prins while I was reading *Have His Carcase* by Dorothy Sayers. This seemed like a bad omen. Thankfully he lived through the trauma.

The seasons of my life have changed over and over and over again. Houses have changed and cities. Each addition of a new child changes the dynamics, and then there are the changes brought about by the subtraction of children. Those are hard changes. That baby bird is so excited to leave the nest, the nest you so carefully constructed for his benefit. What's a mama bird to do? She is going to go on being a human person in her own right. She is no longer connected to her child by that lengthy umbilical cord. The child is free, but so is she. She must learn to embrace that, and the best way to do that is demonstrate her own *joie de vivre* in life. A while ago, my eighth child at twenty years old moved into his own place. It was right and good that he did, and it was a little sad too. Of course, I had been through the process before. I did not cry for a week like I did when my oldest son joined the Navy at nineteen, or even for the twenty-four hours I cried when my second son headed into Hurricane Katrina at nineteen to be a police officer. I still cried though. It was like most of life's changes, bittersweet. What I also did, however, was run to Sherwin-Williams, buy a gallon of Quicksilver paint, and paint his room, thankful he had taken that massive stag's head off the wall when he left. My granddaughters refused to walk upstairs lest that stag jump down and stab them with his horns. I sent them a picture of the new crisp grey and blue room with its white sheers. They replied back, "Oooooh! So pretty, Cici!" It is their room now—and yours. It is a guest room.

> She is going to go on being a human person in her own right.

Well, at least it was a guest room. In one of those inexplicably happy circumstances that come into the life of a woman who loves her children, my son, now well into his twenties, moved back in this summer. We left up the pretty white curtains, and he did not put the stag back up, but nevertheless, he has been home for a respite. A respite for whom? For me. This summer when he says, "Do you want to watch *Loki* with me?" I do not quibble about all the work on my plate, the books to write , or the classes to lead. I just plop myself right down and soak up an hour with my son. Change, and then change again. That is what it means to be a woman.

Time and Morning Time

It is hard not to be trite these days. Even the most sacred things have been oversold and overwrought. Time management is discussed on almost every internet site. Structuring our days has become a top priority in a world full of detours and rabbit trails. We know that we are supposed to go to bed early and get up early. We should exercise, drink water, and avoid social media. I had spent a lifetime developing routines that worked for me and my family. As my family grew up, the routines needed little tweaking. They worked just as well for me alone as they did for a houseful of kids. I savored my mornings, my Morning Time, my coffee, my Bible, poetry, reading, Shakespeare, staring out the window at the lovely changing seasons, and getting in my 10,000 steps.

And then I went to work. Not only did Alex, my youngest, have to be at school by 7:15 a.m., but I had to be at work by 8:30 after a forty-five minute drive. That summer I worked hard on a new schedule that would include all my favorite morning things, and exercise too. This lasted about two weeks. It was hard to go to bed early enough to make this schedule work. If I tried to get in 10,000 steps a day, something else was going to have to give. I couldn't and can't do it all, and I hate that feeling of rushing from one routine to the next in order to check off all the boxes.

Being a mother means I do not know when I will be needed. It is not just lack of discipline that makes my days uncertain; it is the reality of motherhood. And while I do not have nursing babies or unwieldy pregnancies anymore, I have 33 people in my family including my mother in memory care. The unknowns of each day are daunting, even now, when I generally get enough sleep.

Finding what works in new seasons of life is a big deal. Lately I have been returning to what worked for me when my children were small. I cannot control large chunks of my day, but I can control what I do when I have a few minutes. I have to remember not to despise the little moments. I have to remember that ultimately they are all I have or ever will have. I can squander them by getting lost on my phone, or I can use them wisely. Maybe I don't know when or if I will walk 10,000 steps today, but I can walk 100 steps right now while I am waiting for Alex to brush his teeth before we head out the door. If my time seems out of my control, I am more tempted to start binging a show on Netflix. Add up how many hours it took you to binge-watch that mind-numbing show, and it will reveal the time you might have had to read the *Iliad*. I know because I have already done the calculation, and I am appalled at my own ignorance. I am spending my hours buying foolishness, but worse than what I am doing is what I am not doing. It is true that I may have needed an episode or two of *Brooklyn Nine-Nine* to unwind, but four or five episodes? That is not de-stressing, that is paving paradise.

I like concepts of daily rhythms much better than the idea of strict scheduling. Morning Time had a fluidity that allowed it to move into different time slots over the years. The more rigid the schedule the harder it will be to maintain in life's ever changing tides. But to allow life to sweep us along is also a recipe for disaster.

My goal was always 180 Morning Times a year, but I would guess that hitting 90 was what mostly happened. A good year meant that I got in two-thirds of those 180 days, a bad year, half. That's the reality. But look at the numbers. Morning Time is a densely rich time. Ninety days of Morning Time a year was 90 days well spent. In my large family it could have been much worse and sometimes was. Sometimes we had bad days, and sometimes we even had bad years. According to my calculations, one good homeschooling year makes up for two bad ones.

Leisure and Learning

The ancients understood that learning takes place in times of leisure. Only those rich and powerful enough to have leisure had time to learn. It really is just that simple. If I have to go out and kill my meal for the evening or cobble a living making shoes, I am not going to have enough time to learn anything. The ancients spoke of education as "The Liberal Arts." This is a translation of the Latin term *artes liberales*. *Artes* means crafts or skills, and *liberales* comes from *liber*, or free man, an individual who is both politically free, as a citizen with rights, and economically independent, as a member of a wealthy leisure class. In other words, "liberal arts" originally meant something like "skills of the citizen elite" or "skills of the ruling class." Cicero contrasted the *artes libero* (arts worthy of a free man) with the *artes serviles*, the servile arts or lower-class trades.[1] In our modern times some of this has been turned on its

12

head. What once may have been a servile art, like say, making pottery, has now become a visual art or truly just a beautiful art. Skills done well have that added benefit of becoming arts. I like to think that is how God rescues even the lowborn, like me.

In the British TV show *Larkrise to Candleford,* one character, Queenie, speaks about hand making bobbin lace which is a lovely and old art form that was taken over by machines during the Industrial Revolution. This television series takes place in England right after the Industrial Revolution when Queenie's living had been replaced by the factory. Queenie ponders all of this saying, "When I was young all I saw was the purpose of it. Now that it has no purpose, all I see is the beauty of it." Queenie was never free to make bobbin lace. She had to do it in order to live. But when her art was no longer needed, she was finally able to see it for what it was. Utility often blinds us to beauty.

In a nutshell, the liberal arts are for someone who is free (someone at their leisure rather than working to make a living). The opposite of freedom, of course, is slavery. The servile arts were something you had to do in order to survive. So someone in ancient times who had to make money was "servile," while a person who was a property owner or part of the ruling class was free to spend his leisure learning.

Freedom and Slavery

America is a country founded on the ideal of liberty. That means that it is not a country of elite citizens and the masses, like the old feudal models. It is a country where the everyman has an opportunity to be a free man. To be self-governed. The everyman has a chance to understand his fellow man broadly and widely. The liberal arts take on a whole new construct when they are available to all.

David Hicks has a whole chapter in *Norms and Nobility* titled "The Ennobling of the Masses," covering this idea of an elite education for everyone, especially every American.[2] We live in a country based on equality and freedom. Hicks scoffs at the idea that in a free state culture can be cultivated by the few for the many. This creates what I like to call the elite, effete aesthete.

A nobleman used to be someone who owned property. Pericles says in his funeral oration that each one of us is the lord and owner of "his own person." American founding father James Madison says the "conscience is the most sacred property of all,"[3] and Charlotte Mason says that "children are born persons." You could say that we are all property owners. We own ourselves.

Hicks explains this perfectly.

> The logic of democracy demands, however, that everyone be educated as members of an elite. Each student in a democracy must be educated as an aristocrat. Democracy assures him of the unique privileges of an aristocrat. The freedom of thought, expression, movement, and worship, as well as the rights to own property, and to have a voice in framing the laws by which he and his children will be governed.[4]

Hicks goes on to say that technology has given us all the leisure to be "Aristotelean aristocrat[s] . . . by way of universal suffrage."[5] He then describes the responsibilities of the educated human. It is interesting to note that the whole concept of freedom is intimately connected to responsibility. Without responsibility, there is no freedom.

The first responsibility of freedom is in keeping with the role of the mother. The educated mother has a responsibility to the past. I like to call this responsibility remembrance.

Remembrance is an important part of the real trivium, which could be thought of in terms of another trivium: past, present, and future. We are responsible for the past, for remembering.

As parents interested in raising our children as free persons, we forget the past to our detriment. In fact, without knowing the past we can never be free. To be disconnected and unmoored from the past is to be insane, alone, and untethered in the universe. When we forget the past, everything we sense is skewed.

> In fact, without knowing the past we can never be free.

Think about this forgetfulness in terms of taste and remembrance. Even the fruits and vegetables we buy are in the process of forgetting what it means to be, say, a tomato or an ear of corn. The very DNA of these things is in the process of forgetting, as it breaks down and spoils.

Right now, I could go to Publix and buy blackberries. They would be huge, free from bugs, and would not even rot in my fridge. I could make a cobbler, and it might just remind me a little bit of my grandmother's cobbler, and yet this new cobbler with these new, improved berries would also be helping me forget just what a real, wild, natural blackberry tasted like. Without remembrance even our senses are skewed.

After our responsibility to the past, we have five more responsibilities as free, educated humans. Hicks says the educated man has "the obligation to govern himself, to contribute to the preservation of society's values and purpose, a duty to love the law, to respect his fellow man, and to use his leisure for the realization of his marvelous human potentials."[6]

Hicks writes that *paideia,* or education, was "the property of every citizen, a natural right, which he was obligated to practice, to protect, and to pass on."[7] Or one could say that all education is self-education. The self-governed are the self-educated. The freeborn American learner, parent or child, must be educated with elite classical values in order to live out his full potential before God and man and society.

But there is an even broader category of freeborn men. Christians are freeborn.

> Tell me, you who desire to be under the law, do
> you not listen to the law? For it is written that
> Abraham had two sons, one by a slave woman
> and one by a free woman...So, brothers, we are
> not children of the slave but of the free woman.
> (Galatians 4:21-22, 31)

As Americans and as Christians we are entitled to live and move as freeborn people. Owners of our own selves.

Ah, but here is the rub—that word "leisure." It has been my conjecture that homeschooling mothers are the very last vestige of the ancient leisured classes. Homeschooling has in many ways reclaimed the time we need to be educated. Yes, it has stolen from us what is called "free time," but it has given that time to the pursuit of education. Therefore, I propose that we educate our children in ways where we can also repair the ruins, as John Milton wrote,[8] of our own education. That, I think, is the best way to pick a curriculum. Will this curriculum be one where I can learn along with my child or family, or will it push me into the role of family drudge while the children get to do all the learning? Another criteria might be, will this curriculum free up my time so that I can spend the school hours learning alongside my children, albeit maybe something different? This latter criteria is especially helpful for educating older children. Once a mother gets in the habit of daily learning, she will not want to ever give that up. As she ages, she will not only model for others what it means to be freeborn, educated, and self-governed, she will also do well on *Jeopardy!* (I have more than one homeschooling mom friend who was on *Jeopardy!*)

If leisure is so important to learning, then what are the implications for a culture that has become adept at stealing leisure or forfeiting it? That is to say, our treasured free time which gives opportunity for self-education is lost to us, stolen or forfeited through distraction. Tony Reinke, in his book *12 Ways Your Phone is Changing You*, makes the point that we do not have time to *kill*, rather the Bible suggests that we have time to *redeem*. This reminds us of the ideal of remembrance. Our phones and their present distractions steal from us the remembrance of the past while teasing us with the

> Our phones and their distractions steal from us the past while teasing us with the future.

future. Sadly, when we get to the future, we will find that it can't exist in a vacuum.

My other concern with technology is its link to depression. A depressed mom is unable to think and learn. She is mired in her own psyche, and it is a hellish place. I am a firm believer in seeking help for depression, but I also think we can be proactive against it in some ways. Whether it is the social implications of seeing everyone's best side online or the actual negative impact of certain light waves on our brains, moving away from the distraction of the phone is the first line of defense against depression. Even if you are not depressed, spending less time on your device will free up massive amounts of time. Most of us wildly underestimate the time we spend on our devices.

Again, it is not what we are doing, but what we are *not* doing!

> Most of us wildly underestimate the time we spend on our devices. Again, it is not what we are doing, but what we are not doing!

A Woman I Knew: Wendi Capehart

My friend Wendi is not around anymore. I did go to her memorial service so her passing was confirmed, but it is not something my brain has accepted. I think one reason I struggle with this sad fact is that every single day, on the internet or on my bookshelf, I see evidences of Wendi. People who never even knew she existed are impacted by her great mind daily. She left the best kind of legacy—one which she herself never really knew. She was just busy being Wendi Capehart, a beautiful woman made in the image of

God with an enormous IQ. Wendi was truly a thinking woman and one I referred to frequently, without irony, as the smartest woman on the internet.

Clearly, Wendi was given the gift of intelligence, but it's what she did with it that is so fascinating. She didn't pile up degrees or become a university professor; she stayed home, had children, and read, amassing a lot of children and a lot more books along the way. That is where God found her, and that is where He used her. And that is why today thousands of people all over the world owe her a big thank-you for faithfully being Wendi Capehart. And many of them have never even heard her name.

The Ideal and the Reality

During the course of this book I am going to talk about some outstanding lives—women like Wendi. I am going to propose that we take educating ourselves seriously, just as seriously as we take educating our children. I want to set the bar high, yes, but the last thing I want to do is cause you to be discouraged. I know from experience that reading Proverbs 31 can be discouraging. How in the world am I going to go buy a field and sell it?

What I will be showing you in this book is a life. The big picture. What can be, if you are faithful with the little things. If you don't despise the day of small things, you don't really have to worry about the big picture on a day-to-day basis. Most days won't look or feel like they are adding up to much. That is the beauty of life in Christ. We do our part, and God gives the increase. In my book *Mere Motherhood*, I describe how God sent me a job homeschooling other people's children at the end of my own homeschooling career. I did not go looking for this job. It came to me, and it utilized all my strengths. I have seen this happen for other mothers too.

The life of faith is not complicated. It is not easy either. Our job is to be faithful in the small things and not worry about the outcome. Isn't it interesting how easy it is to focus on the outcome we want when we plan our life? Isn't it interesting how often that life goes awry? That is why I advise not getting ahead of yourself. We cannot know the future or the outcomes of our choices. We can only faithfully and prayerfully live each day looking unto Jesus who is the author and finisher of it all.

Many young moms despair because they have given up everything the world deems important to raise children. Culturally, there is not a pat on the back in sight. You have to faithfully work in the fields of your home and family without any encouragement while being vilified by the culture and often family members. How has the world gotten to a place where the most important job of all is the least admired? It is not a glamorous job, with its spit-up and peanut butter stains. It is a life of almost non-stop self-denial. Even the people you are denying yourself for will never really know the price you paid to do it. It would be easy to let this reduce you to a depressed, self-pitying person. This happens when we lose our self-respect in the face of a daunting lack of appreciation. Don't. Don't go down that road.

Educating yourself while you spend your days with your children will bring the highest dividends. Put on self-confidence and warmth as you wake up each morning ready to homeschool both your children and yourself. Don't worry about that atta-girl yet.

Seek first God's kingdom, recognize your place as a daughter in His palace, and give each day your best. Some days your best will be just keeping everybody from killing each other. Other days will gloriously hint at those future rewards. The King of the universe has given you a subversive, undercover mission. Hold your head high even when your hair is dirty.

Try not to look at all the days you don't achieve your goals, but rather, be encouraged by how many days you do reach your goals. Don't measure failure. We all fail in many ways. The key to dealing with failure is to brazen it out. The wise and wonderful Winston Churchill was believed to have said, "If you are going through hell, keep going."[9] This was a man who understood failure. We often think of Churchill as the man who saved western civilization from the Nazis, and he did. He was a brilliant, dogged man. But he was also a man who had faced more failure and setbacks than most of us could handle.

During World War I, he was ousted as First Lord of the Admiralty because his proposed battle plan for the Dardanelles ended up costing the Allies 46,000 men. We know it as the Battle of Gallipoli.[10] He also faced days which he called black-dog depression days, perhaps from bearing the weight of the world on his shoulders. To a mom, your family is the weight of the world. Many moms face depression, set-backs, and outright failure. You were not meant to bear these burdens. In the next chapter, I hope to encourage you to seek first God's kingdom.

Suggested Reading

The Mind of the Maker by Dorothy Sayers

The Pursuit of God by A. W. Tozer

The Knowledge of the Holy by A. W. Tozer

The Pursuit of Holiness by Jerry Bridges

The Roots of American Order by Russell Kirk

Norms and Nobility by David Hicks

Never Give In: The Extraordinary Character of Winston Churchill by Stephen Mansfield

My Early Life: 1874-1904 by Winston S. Churchill

Liturgy of the Ordinary by Tish Warren

12 Ways Your Phone is Changing You by Tony Reinke

Growth Ideas

- Listen to Churchill's "Never Give In" speech on YouTube.
- Watch the movie *The Darkest Hour* (2017).
- Set up a Morning Time for your family or yourself. (My book *Morning Time: A Liturgy of Love* can get you started.)

CHAPTER TWO

The Contemplative Mother

> Whenever you read the Gospel, Christ Himself is
> speaking to you. And while you read, you are praying
> and talking to Him.
>
> St. Tikhon of Zadonsk
>
> The man who would truly know God must give time
> to Him.
>
> A. W. Tozer

God's Word

I almost hate to start this chapter so early in the book, but Bible
reading is the single most important thing I am going to write
about. When this book is finished, if you only take one thing
away, I hope it is the realization that spending time in God's Word
is the best way you can spend your time. Before you start to feel
guilty, let me explain that I am not talking about spending time in
God's Word because you SHOULD. I am saying, if someone handed you a simple key to unlock wisdom and virtue and a glimpse of
the loving Creator who made you, a key that would change every
room you entered for the better, would you ask them if you HAD
to use it?

Education is the ordering of our loves. The Bible is the tool that
will help us sort out what we should love from what we shouldn't
love. No, I am not talking about rock music and backward masking

(the theory that musicians were secretly encoding messages in their music tracks which could be heard if you played them backwards, as if we didn't have enough trouble with normal lyrics). Surprisingly, we will find very few dos and don'ts in the Bible. Remember when we talked about liberty in the first chapter? The Bible is a book that explains how free people live. It doesn't steal that freedom.

Among all of life's uncertainties, I can make one promise to you. If you read God's Word faithfully, you will come to love it. It is completely and utterly lovable. It is intimate and personal. It is a love letter from God to you. More than loving the Bible, though, because ultimately that is not the real goal, the Bible will help you to know God, the Creator. When you come to know God through His Word then you will have no choice but to love Him.

More than loving the Bible though, because ultimately that is not the real goal, the Bible will help you to know God, the Creator.

For many of you, loving God seems like a chore, a duty. That is exactly how I used to feel. I wanted to love God, and I tried to love Him, but He seemed very obscure. Being a firstborn girl with a propensity for rule-following, and having grown up in a church founded by A. B. Simpson,[1] that patron saint of loving God, I dutifully began having my "devotions" in high school. I could see that my parents read their Bibles every day, and as I moved toward adulthood, I imitated them. This single act of duty on my part, year after year after year—and let me say the years are adding up quickly—finally became such an entrenched part of my life that today I would be devastated if I could not read my Bible in the mornings. What started as a duty ended as the single most important part of my life.

Several things happened because I just kept reading. First, I memorized vast portions of Scripture without even trying. (Just don't ask me for chapter and verse.) Second, I started seeing how intimately connected to me God was through His Word. Third, I began to love the Bible and finally, I began to love God. This led me to a life of praying without ceasing. Just like Bible reading, praying ceased to be a duty; it became the very essence of my life. Bible reading led me to stop talking about the Bible and its demands all the time to my children and start just living a Spirit-filled life. This freed both me and my children. Unfortunately, this was a long time coming for me.

None of this is to say that I am now a sinless person who never makes mistakes because I have the Holy Spirit. *Au contraire.* If only. But I do know what to do with my agonizingly terrible sins, even sins that have harmed both me and my family. I take them to Jesus. I do not wallow in them, giving them power over me. They have no power. I am full of sin, but Christ has figured all that out. As the song says, "He who knows me best, loves me most."[2]

Over the years, I have read the Bible in a myriad of ways. When I was nineteen, I picked up my paternal grandmother's old copy of *Halley's Bible Handbook.* Halley suggested reading three chapters in the Old Testament a day and two in the New Testament to get through the Old Testament in one year and the New Testament twice a year. I have done this plan several times since then, mostly before I had children and now as my nest is almost empty. There is something critical in reading the Bible through, and no matter how I am reading the Bible or what plan I am using, I try to keep reading it through. Reading the Bible through can take three months or even three years or longer. It isn't a race.

I have noticed two trends in Christian circles lately. First, there is the trend to admit you never read the Bible. This is the kind of authenticity this generation strives for. Even mature Christian women find themselves admitting this. It makes me sad. Sad for them. Sad for all the soundness of life and love that they are missing. It also makes them vulnerable to bad doctrine (and there is a lot of that going around). When I say bad doctrine, I do not mean the denominational distinctives, which we all have, but the kind of doctrine that veers away from our foundational beliefs as stated by C. S. Lewis in *Mere Christianity*, or the Apostles' or Nicene Creeds. Can you be a Christian and not read your Bible? Absolutely, but why? Why would you do that? It's your loss, and it's a big one.

The second trend is the idea that Bible study is complicated. We take out our Matthew Henry commentary and Strong's Concordance, and we labor over every little word. We buy devotionals and come up with complicated programs for study. We put these all out on a table, grab a cup of coffee (and it better be a strong cup of espresso), and take a picture for Instagram. We spend one day in the intense study of some word in the Bible like, say, "dwell," a word I happen to like very much, and then we crash and burn. The next morning the oatmeal burns, and the baby has smeared poop in his crib, and the older children are hitting one another in spite of that rule you made about no touching, and there are not two minutes left for your big giant Bible plan. And that is the end of that.

In my recent speaking engagements, I have been doing a little exercise. I ask everyone to turn in their Bibles to John chapter one. Then I set the timer for one minute and ask everyone to start reading. At the end of one minute I say, "Stop," and we see how far we have gotten. It averages fifteen to twenty verses. In one minute a day, you can read fifteen verses of the Bible! Even the most overwhelmed of us has one minute. We spend more time than that scrolling online. If you have time to get on Facebook or Instagram, you have time to read your Bible. There are 31,102 verses in the Bible. If you only read fifteen verses a day, it would take you 2,073 days to read through the Bible. That is a little under six years. If you have not read through the Bible in the last six years, you might want to try this. If you only read your Bible for one minute a day for a lifespan of Bible reading of say, sixty years, you could read through the Bible ten times. If you are having trouble fitting in Bible reading, it might help if you stopped thinking about it as a big project and rather looked at it as something you can do in small chunks. After all, you probably have a Bible app on your phone.

I try to make sure that Bible reading is the first thing I do every day. I am not always successful. Sometimes I peek at my email, check social media, or play Wordle before I even get out of bed, but as a rule, if I have time for social media, then I have time for Bible reading.

Bible Reading

As much as I love my Bible reading, it doesn't always feel wonderful, as if God was speaking to me personally. Sometimes it just feels like a bunch of genealogies. Sometimes I do it because. But that BECAUSE has been a big part of consistently reading over the course of my life. Perhaps it isn't the best reason, but in the end it is the one that has brought me the most fruit. Faithfully plodding through almost anything year after year will bring some fruit, but faithfully plodding through the Bible will bring the most and best fruit.

I am not saying never spend time digging deeper into the Word, but I am saying there are seasons for digging deeper. Every season is the time to read God's Word.

If you do want to read through the Bible a little bit at a time, there are some great reading plans. My favorite is the M'Cheyne one-year daily reading plan. It keeps both the Psalms and the Gospels in constant rotation, so that you get through the Psalms and New Testament twice a year and the Old Testament once. I also like the ESV Plan which has four sections daily: the Psalms and Wisdom Literature, Pentateuch and History of Israel, Chronicles and Prophets, and the Gospels and Epistles.[3]

I will discuss reading the Psalms more when we get to suffering and pain.

Hiding God's Word in your heart will not make your family life perfect, but you will know where to turn when things go badly awry. The thread of Scripture running through your heart will always provide hope, even in the darkest hours. We will talk more about suffering later, but every single person reading this book will face suffering in their lives. The key to hope is knowing God and believing him.

The key to that is having His Word hidden in your heart.

A few years ago, I participated in a Kickstarter program for a beautiful app called Dwell. It is a soothing audio Bible app which gives you a choice of voices and lots of different plans, such as "40 Days with Paul," "Reading through the Psalms," or "Benedictions and Doxologies." They have turned the Bible into playlists of the most lovely type, all with peaceful background selections. I love using the Book of Common Prayer morning and evening playlists daily. I love falling asleep to Rosie from Australia on 1.3 speed. In fact, it has solved my struggles to fall asleep, and I even sometimes use the sleep playlists in the middle of the night if I wake up with anxiety.

It is not the cheapest app out there, but I am finding it to be one of the loveliest.

Meditation: The Hours and Prayer

The idea of meditation is popular these days. Our addiction to the online community and the ever present escapism of our phones make that inevitable. People who have no religious beliefs whatsoever find comfort in separating the practice of prayer and meditation from a Supreme Being. Thus we have all kinds of meditation apps available to us.

We are unable to withstand the onslaught of idea after idea coming our way without a break.

Humans need down time. Away time. Quiet time. We are unable to withstand the onslaught of idea after idea coming our way without a break. Many of us are breaking down altogether. For some of us, even the very light of our phones is hurting our brains. We were not meant to be over-stimulated.

When my eighth child was born, he came into a family who loved him dearly. If I hadn't been nursing him, I might have never seen him. Even when I put him down for a nap, I would look up and someone would be carrying him around. "He was crying," they would explain. After a while, I noticed he would not always make eye contact. Finally, after much worry on my part, I realized that this little guy was overstimulated. He needed a break from so much love. When his brain was overstimulated, he shut down and refused to look at us. After I realized that, I was able to provide him with more rest and quiet time. I was more careful with baby number nine.

As with most of life, organic growth is closely tied to disciplined habits.

Meditation and prayer are two of the great traditions of Christianity and are closely related to each other. In some ways, as you become closer and closer to God in your walk with him, you will naturally begin to pray and meditate, but in other ways, these are disciplines we need to cultivate. As with most of life, organic growth is closely tied to disciplined habits.

As a mother of a large family, the idea of habits always discouraged me. I felt overwhelmed even thinking of trying to bring order to the chaos of our lives. It turned out that habits helped us in spite of it all. Organically, we developed routines and habits in our home and ultimately those habits, such as regular morning routines and Morning Time, saved us. In the same way, just thinking about having to meditate can make us crazy. The more I try to meditate, the worse I feel. Once again, the key is to start small. Don't try to meditate for twenty minutes. Try one or two minutes.

Just being quiet and breathing will make you physically healthier.

My sister recommended the book *Emotionally Healthy Spirituality* by Peter Scazzero to me a couple of years ago, and the book was a perfect beginner's manual for practicing some of the older spiritual disciplines. I was not totally unfamiliar with these disciplines. When I was in high school, my parents had read *The Celebration of Discipline* by Richard Foster, and I had read it too, even swiping it from their shelves when I left home. (I was one of those indiscriminate youthful readers. I also read my mother's copy of *The Total Woman* by Marabel Morgan. Don't ask!)

A few years ago, I asked my sister, Jody, if she would like to read *Emotionally Healthy Spirituality Day by Day* by Peter Scazzero along with me. The book is divided up into forty days of morning and evening meditations. We decided to only read one a day, thus taking us eighty days to finish. We would text each other on days when the devotional was especially helpful or even when we disagreed with Scazzero. My favorite part of the whole journey was that before and after each meditation, Scazzero suggests setting a timer and breathing for two minutes.[4] I would sit in my living room after having my regular Bible time, pick up the daily reading, and ask Alexa to set a timer for two minutes. ("No, Alexa, TWO minutes, not ten." I finally learned to over-pronounce the word "two" for her.) But those two minutes, followed by two more at the end of the very short reading, became the highlight of my day. I loved those minutes. I longed for them. When Jody and I finished the book, I was sad. I wish there were more books like that. As easy as breathing and setting a timer with Alexa is, one would think I do it regularly, but I have not faithfully done that since being directed by the devotional. Writing this reminds me that I can do that tomorrow morning before my daily reading or right now. Yes, I can do it right now, and so can you.

Okay, I am back. Just as you can meditate for two minutes at a time using a timer, you can also pray for two minutes at a time. Two minutes begins to feel like a long time when you are praying. You can pray for all kinds of things. We usually pray as we go for those things that press on us and worry us, but this more rigid, timed prayer can be used for those things you might forget to pray for—like sick friends, extended family members with special problems, the government and rulers in authority, or your church and its leaders. Praying is a special gift that God gives us. It is how he allows us to participate in all the wonderful things he is doing in the world.

While preparing to give a talk on the habit of attention, I came across one reason why attention is so important for both our children and ourselves as I read *Beauty in the Word* by Stratford Caldecott. Caldecott makes the case that prayer is turning our attention to God.[5] That is why it is to be done without ceasing. Our hearts, when they truly find their home, will constantly turn their attention that way. Caldecott quotes Simone Weil in saying that the reason attention is so important in education, and we know that Charlotte Mason emphasized attention also, is that prayer consists of attention. All of our educational studies, where we learn to pay attention, train us to pray. Caldecott says that growth in prayer is at the heart of education. If that is so, what are the implications for a generation with extremely short attention spans? Without attention, we have no prayer. This is where retraining our mind to pay attention for two minutes is vital to our growth as humans and as Christians. We must train our children in the habit of attention, and we must retrain ourselves in this habit. Slowly, two minutes at a time.

The Book of Common Prayer is a big help in these endeavors, but it is often a mystery to those of us who have not grown up reading it. Recently, in a used book store, I ran across a few volumes by Phyllis Tickle which make the prayer book more accessible to me. These beautifully crafted volumes are called *The Divine Hours,* and they are divided by season. In each volume, Tickle practices three of what is known as the Liturgy of the Hours or the Divine Office.

Traditionally, the canonical hours have been divided like this:

> Matins (during the night or at midnight, also
>   called Vigils or Nocturns)
> Lauds (the dawn hour or 3 a.m.)
> Prime (the first hour, 6 a.m.)
> Terce (the third hour, 9 a.m.)
> Sext (the sixth hour, noon)
> None (the ninth hour, 3 p.m.)
> Vespers (Evensong, 6 p.m.)
> Compline (before bed, 9 p.m.)

It is fun to know these because they often show up in English literature, and even murder mysteries, like those of Dorothy Sayers and Ellis Peters. It is nice to know that while these give a beautiful order to life and days as practiced by monks, it is hardly possible for us to duplicate them, unless we are nursing a newborn. Then we will find they correspond almost exactly to the baby's feeding times. Perhaps it would be more romantic to think of the 3 a.m. feeding as Lauds.

Phyllis Tickle divides the time of reading and prayer into only three parts: The Morning Office (6-9 a.m.), the Midday Office (11 a.m.-2 p.m.), and the Vespers Office (5-8 p.m.). Most of her sections cover several components: Scripture readings in small portions (from the Old Testament, New Testament, and Psalms), weekly prayers, the Gloria Patri, the Lord's Prayer, and even some hymns.[6]

As much as I would love to divide my days into these three parts and turn my mind formally towards God and His church and the community of saints, I can barely make it through one or two sections a day. This means that on some mornings, I am reading an evening Vespers.

> I am following my usual pattern to get through any schedule— plodding.

I am following my usual pattern to get through any schedule—plodding. I am plodding my way through the hours. Edith Schaeffer says that if you want all or nothing you get nothing, and I have made that the motto of my life.[7] I order everything by the principle that a little is better than nothing. You will see this concept of plodding throughout this book. It is the heart of what I am trying to say. One key to plodding is always picking up where you left off. If you are behind, do not try to catch up by going back and reading extra on a given day. Just keep reading. It might take you three years to get through a one-year devotional, but that is better than not getting through anything at all. Just keep plodding.

There has been a renewal in recent years of turning towards even older monastic practices than the prayer book. The *Rule of*

St. Benedict (c. 593) has become increasingly popular. Benedict of Nursia's rule provided the principles for communal living for the monks. One reason monastic life and worship resonate with us is that they cover all the mundane ordinary parts of living. Esther de Waal's little book *Seeking God* is a great place to start for those interested in applying these ideas in our own time and context. I love how Esther makes it clear that her book is for ordinary Christians, not just monks. As I have been reading de Waal, I have been reminded once again of the beauty of the life of the stay-at-home mom. Who else in our culture is ordering their days in both the mundane and the sacred? Not only are moms at home fulfilling the ancient ideal of *scholé*, they are also fulfilling the sacred life of order and worship found in monasteries all across medieval Europe. That dirty diaper is an icon to the lowly way you have chosen, the giving and caring for life created by God Himself.

No wonder you are scorned and derided by our culture. You are a seriously dangerous threat to the status quo. The iconoclasts don't want your dirty diapers, or your sweet babies, or your ordered days. They will exchange all of that for thirty pieces of silver, which you can then use to buy some of that STUFF you saw on Pinterest or Instagram. Just trade in the laundry and the dishes and the constant toil for money, and you will have treasure on earth. Without faith, it is impossible to see through this exchange. Nobody will tell you about the moths and the rust or the fact that once you drive that new car off the lot it is already diminished. Before you can walk out the door with that iPhone 13, the iPhone 15 is in the store. You have to have faith in God to recognize the lie and to believe you are storing up treasure in Heaven. That begins in the most mundane tasks you do each day. Monasticism reminds us of this. But it is not all drudgery, as some would have you believe. You can pray for that new car or that new porch furniture or that vacation. I do. God hears all those prayers you send up to Him. After you pray, monasticism reminds us again of what comes next—waiting. Praying and waiting are marks of trust. Praying and waiting with a smile, and not frustration, is the hallmark of joy. When we understand in our heart of hearts that we can trust God completely, then we will find joy.

Other Devotional Materials

If you get to the place in your life where you are consistently reading God's Word daily, you can also begin reading other devotional materials. I especially like to read older devotionals because they remind me of what other Christians in the past thought. This is in keeping with C. S. Lewis's advice to always read an old book after a new one. It is important for us to keep a perspective on our own times and groupthink by looking to the past.

My favorite devotional of all time is *Morning and Evening* by Charles Spurgeon. If I need some solid truth, he is the go-to guy. If you are a Catholic, I would skip him, though, as he also was infected by the times he lived in and therefore is not a fan of the Pope. If you do read Spurgeon, remember, if you can understand that people live in their own times, it will save you from becoming a politically correct ignoramus, only able to read things you agree with. Moderns are so quick and so arrogant to throw out things from the past because we are so much wiser in our own eyes. This phenomenon scares me. There is not a book that I recommend that I don't have some reservations about or some minor or major disagreement with. Being a discerning reader allows you the freedom to graze in many pastures. Wheat and chaff.

Once again, as I suggested with the Divine Office, I recommend using Spurgeon's devotional your way. You might read "Morning" devotions one year and "Evening" the next, if twice a day doesn't fit your situation. You don't have to read it every morning and evening. You can even read April 14 on January 1. Just read the next thing. I read both "Morning" and "Evening" devotions in the mornings whenever I am reading *Morning and Evening*. I have found the evenings much less flexible with my schedule.

Tim and Kathy Keller have written several devotionals, including my favorite yearly one on the Psalms called *The Songs of Jesus*. I recently purchased one on Proverbs titled *God's Wisdom for Navigating Life*. I hope to begin it next year.

A few years ago, after my Bible reading, I read *A Year with C. S. Lewis: Daily Readings from His Classic Works*. I have a policy of reading at least one, and usually several, volumes of Lewis each year, in the hope that I might someday read all of his writings. This book is a nice remembrance of some of his great passages.

Other great devotionals are *Streams in the Desert* by Mrs. Charles Cowman, which I highly recommend for times of suffering and stress, and *My Utmost for His Highest* by Oswald Chambers, which I recommend taking with a grain of salt. I find Mr. Chambers to be a bit of a stern legalist at times.

I love devotionals so much because they fit nicely into my philosophy of small things. I hope one day to write one myself. Most devotionals can be read in less than five minutes a day. They are a perfect addition to the liturgical life. Just remember there are many seasons of a mother's life when she cannot add anything at all to her time besides Bible reading. Those seasons are real. Just be careful to pay attention when things loosen up and you do have time again. Not being aware of the changing seasons of life is often where bad habits develop.

I have also recently discovered devotionals by Sinclair Ferguson. They are short and deep. Perfect for busy women.

Sabbath

My friend, Angelina Stanford, used to write about the Sabbath in a family's life on her blog. I had been thinking of the Sabbath too, and her thoughts were helpful. There are many ways we can think of Sabbath, and I don't think it is any more or less important these days than it ever was. Sabbath is tied to the creation. The Creator rested on the seventh day. It starts in the beginning. It is crucial that we understand this, or we might think of it as some major DON'TS given to us in the Ten Commandments. It is, of course, a major commandment, but it is based on the creation. We are creatures designed for sabbath rest. Sabbath is not a rule, but a gift. We can use sabbath in the traditional way by setting aside one day a week for God, and we can also think of it more broadly as it applies to all of our routines, plans, and even addictions. We enjoy returning to our daily routine when we take a break from it. Taking a sabbath break from Facebook or Instagram can break us of letting those things take

> Not being aware of the changing seasons of life is often where bad habits develop.

up too much of our time and emotional energy. Anything that vies for supremacy in our lives is a good place to practice sabbath. Sabbath gives us a chance to evaluate the things we spend our time on. Maybe it just gives us a fresh perspective. I think it is the best tool for freshening our perspectives. While I clearly love good habits, I have also learned that habits themselves need sabbath. In fact, this year I coined a new maxim: "A habit needs a sabbath."

The most basic way of keeping sabbath in your life is through church attendance. Church attendance doesn't always feel good. Sometimes it almost feels like drudgery. It is strangely out-of-sync with our post-post-modern lives. When we do go to church, we have unrealistic expectations about what church life should look like. We want community, and we want it now. We have read all the books. We long for community, and then we head out the door to church expecting instant connection. When our churches fail to provide this, we move along to the next church, or we just stop going altogether. I have thought long and hard about community. If there is one thing our forebears had that we do not have, it is time. Oh, they had the same amount of actual time that we have, but they often spent all of their time in one place. They had a sense of place. My favorite writings of Wendell Berry center on place, especially in his book *The Art of the Commonplace*. But place and time are entwined. How can something become "commonplace" without time?

When we moved to Chattanooga and looked for a church, I decided to do an experiment. This experiment was based on a lifetime of frustration in looking for PLACE, especially in a church community. I decided, after we settled on our home church of North

Shore Fellowship, to not get impatient to get to know people, not to feel unloved or uncared for because I didn't know anyone at church. I decided to be okay with taking my time in developing relationships. The experiment was to sit there for ten years, participate as I was able and called to, but not to worry about where I fit in or stress over the fact that I am shy and awkward. I wanted to see if I would eventually grow into the church organically. Over ten years later, I can say that I have. My place at church seems to me now to be a living, organic thing, unforced and natural. I am still a shy, awkward person in real life and at church, but I have eventually fit in at church anyway, although I still hyperventilate when we have that awful greet-one-another time in the middle of the service. But even that reminds me that it is okay to be awkward.

Our spiritual, emotional, and even physical health all thrive on routine and a break from routine, sabbath.

This experiment has taught me that we probably didn't give some churches a chance to be "our" church in the past. Sticking with a church might be the soundest way to grow into organic community. Sticking with it for a long, long time. Do you want your children to be gracious to you someday when they see all your mistakes? Be gracious today with your church. Your children will learn more about real community when you stay rather than leave.

After church attendance, we can apply sabbath by setting apart the rest of the day to do things outside of our routines or even ideally, using sabbath to remember our Creator. We must have routine, and we must have sabbath. Routine doesn't work without sabbath. Our spiritual, emotional, and even physical health all thrive on routine and a break from routine, sabbath. Sometimes it is even healthy in families to have breaks from one another. I know that children probably listen to mom more when they get a break from her voice.

Women I Knew: Carol Conn and Helen Rollins

In my lifetime, I have known two women who walked almost completely by faith. At least it seemed that way from my perspective, although I am quite sure neither one of them considered herself a spiritual giant. The one was Carol Conn, a Christian and Missionary Alliance Missionary to Ecuador, and the other was my mother-in-law, Helen Rollins.

Carol exhibited a spirit of cheerfulness and trust contrary to her life's circumstances. She had a way of loving the most unlovable people. She didn't go around spouting wisdom, but if you ever once met her, you somehow knew you had met a person who walked with God. She was the epitome of a gentle and quiet spirit. I Peter 3:4 describes her exactly.

> But let it be the hidden person of the heart, with the imperishable quality of a gentle and quiet spirit, which is precious in the sight of God. (NASB)

Carol Conn was a hidden person, precious in the sight of God. Elisabeth Elliot writes about her time with Carol when Elisabeth went to Ecuador for the first time to see Jim. Even Elisabeth Elliot, a giant in her own right, recognized Carol's unique spiritual gifts of gentleness and quietness.

Helen Rollins was not always quite so gentle. She was southern born and southern bred, which meant she and her sisters could dish it out and take it. It was fun to watch them do it. You wouldn't want to miss one of their church dinners either, unless you were on a diet. Helen's life was not an easy one. At times she raised her large family in church basements, including snakes, with no money for food. The children often ate ground beef with flour gravy or even just plain biscuits. She must have learned a lot about trust as she scrounged for food for her family while her husband preached and invited people over to dinner, without once thinking that maybe there wasn't any dinner to share.

Her hardscrabble life reminds me of Susannah Wesley, Christian mother of many, who said:

> I never did want for bread. But then, I had so much care to get it before it was eaten, and to pay for it after, it has often made it very unpleasant to me.[8]

That is where faith is born, isn't it? Not in all those idyllic moments of joy, but faith is born in harder soil.

Helen had a simple faith that meant one thing: a life of prayer. She prayed for her family. She never had the money to travel much to see her large family after they grew up. We often only saw her once every couple of years. But whenever we talked to her on the phone, she reminded us that she was praying for us. I didn't share with her all the struggles I faced over the years when I was pregnant or nursing, but she had borne six children, and she knew. Just when I felt I was about to be overwhelmed and washed away by life, she would call and tell me she was praying for me. By the end of my childbearing years, I clung to her prayers, like a drowning man to a raft. When I couldn't pray, she could. When I had no faith, she did. When she died, I felt like a giant black hole opened in the universe. Who was going to pray now? Well, it was obvious. I was going to have to step up to the plate.

The Ideal and the Reality

I have given you lots of ideas in this chapter, and if you tried to do them all at once you would fail. I don't do any of these things all at the same time except plodding away at reading my Bible and continually turning to God in prayer. If you knew my two ideal spiritual mentors, Carol and Helen, during their lives you would see that they also failed to do it all. Both were women of the Word and prayer, but neither managed to reach sinless perfection. Happily, they are now resting from their labors in Heaven, and I am pretty sure that means they have no regrets. Jesus paid it all. "There is therefore now no condemnation for those who are in Christ Jesus."[9] Just because we can't reach the ideal in this life, doesn't mean it is not good, though. Women have a tendency to get defensive in the face of the ideal. I know I do. But we don't have to. When we see people doing better than us in some area, we can rejoice. We can train ourselves to love those weaker and those stronger than ourselves. By letting go of defensiveness, we allow ourselves the freedom to grow. We don't have to have arrived. We can be on the journey.

Two of the most encouraging—and most helpful to modern women—concepts in the Benedictine tradition are stability and balance. Ecclesiastes reminds us that there is a time for everything.

If we are feeling harried and overwhelmed, it might be good to remind ourselves to slow down. Not to run too far ahead. As mothers not ruled by the cultural forces, at least in theory, we are able to break through the lies we are fed. While having a rigid schedule is dangerous, not paying attention to the rhythms of life is equally so. A rigid schedule is saying that you want all or nothing. A rhythm is accepting the flow of life with grace, while putting into practice those habits which promote mental, physical, and spiritual health. Rarely does our health benefit from extremes. This is where balance comes in. If you are feeling anxious or overwhelmed, one area to examine is balance. Where are you chasing extremes in your life? Modern social media pushes us toward extremes. No matter what our interest, Pinterest will always show you ways to exploit it. So examine your life for those things which are disordered or overdone. A wide and generous life is the healthiest life.

My own life usually frustrates me when I try to implement health measures that are extreme and therefore impossible. Unrealistic reading goals can put the cart before the horse. I may not want to read that long Barbara Tuchman book if it slows down my book count for the year. How silly is that? But that is how quickly something good can get off balance. As we continue through this book, I will bring up balance and stability again and again. They are just that important.

> A rhythm is accepting the flow of life with grace, while putting into practice those habits which promote mental, physical, and spiritual health.

Suggested Reading

The Bible

Mere Christianity by C. S. Lewis

Emotionally Healthy Spirituality by Peter Scazzero

Emotionally Healthy Spirituality Day by Day by Peter Scazzero

Beauty in the Word by Stratford Caldecott

The Divine Hours by Phyllis Tickle

Seeking God: The Way of St. Benedict by Esther de Waal

Morning and Evening by Charles Spurgeon

My Utmost for His Highest by Oswald Chambers

Streams in the Desert by Mrs. Charles Cowman

The Songs of Jesus by Timothy and Kathy Keller

God's Wisdom for Navigating Life by Timothy and Kathy Keller

A Year With C. S. Lewis: Daily Readings from His Classic Works by C. S. Lewis, edited by Patricia S. Klein

The Art of the Commonplace by Wendell Berry

The Praying Life by Paul E. Miller

To Seek and to Save: Daily Reflections on the Road to the Cross and other devotionals by Sinclair Ferguson

Growth Ideas

Try using a smart phone app for a devotional aid.

- YouVersion has the Scriptures in different versions as well as devotional resources.
- Dwell: audio Bible app that has been helpful for me.

- Daily Prayer, my favorite app using the Book of Common Prayer.

I like several read-through-the-Bible plans:

- Robert Murray M'Cheyne's plan
- The ESV Reading Plan
- If you have a lot of time to read the Bible, try Dr. Horton's plan.

CHAPTER THREE

The Reading Mother

You can never get a cup of tea large enough or a book
long enough to suit me.

C. S. Lewis

Reading

Reading—has there ever been anything more at the heart of
self-education than reading? Reading is the lifeblood of self-education. Readers are leaders, we are told, and I like to think that
is true. The time invested in reading will bring lifelong rewards. I
was born into a culture of reading. My parents bought books and
read books. They bought books for me too. I was rather surprised
to hear my dad say that he was not a reader in his younger days, as I
had never seen him without a book by his side. When I was young,
those volumes were coaching and motivational books, and often
biographies, because he was a baseball coach. But as he grew older,
they were more devotional in nature. He introduced me, and my
children, to Eugene H. Peterson and his lovely book *Run With
the Horses* about Jeremiah and the book of Lamentations. Peterson
reminds us that Jeremiah probably wrote, "God's mercies are new
every morning," from the pit they had thrown him in. While my
dad was in the hospital, several old ball players dropped in, and
more than one of them mentioned *The Pursuit of God* by A. W.

Tozer to remind my dad of his impact on their lives. He coached D1 baseball—these were not Christian schools, and yet my dad's unassuming testimony spoke volumes.

My parents weren't wealthy, and they weren't intellectuals. But they were readers. You could say they became readers. Even though my dad didn't think of himself as a reader, he was because he read. A reader is someone who reads.

Many of you did not grow up in an atmosphere of reading. Your homes were not always lacking bookshelf space; none was needed. If this is you, you may be wondering how to create a life of reading. Recently, Goodreads ran an article about some of the people who logged the most books in a year.[1] The stories of each super-reader were familiar. Heavy readers read along the way. They had books by their beds and books in their cars and books in their purses. The worst nightmare for a reader is to find oneself somewhere like the DMV without a book. (Scrolling a phone is just not the same thing, unless you happen to have a Kindle app. I once read *The Idiot* by Dostoevsky on my phone at the DMV). My first Stephen King book was not *Carrie* or *The Stand*, books I still haven't the stomach for, but rather his wonderful book on the writing life, *On Writing: A Memoir of the Craft*. King says that if you want to write then you must read. Part of his preparation for writing is to be always reading. He even uses audiobooks in his car in order to read more. King, an English teacher born to an English teacher, loves English words. In his novel *11.23.62*, he loves the word "obdurate" obdurately. It comforts me to know that even King needs an editor sometimes.

> [Stephen] King says that if you want to write then you must read.

In order to be a reader, you just have to read. Once again, the theme of this book shines through. You don't have to read a whole book today. If you want to be a reader, you just have to read *something*. I read *War and Peace* a paragraph at a time before bed for several years. It was soporific, but I have fond memories of it still.

Reading for Pleasure

Can reading for pure pleasure contribute to lifelong learning? Of course it can. To me this seems like a no-brainer, but over the years I have met many people who feel that reading fiction is an unproductive waste of time. Even in my own family, different people have different preferences for pleasure reading. My son Nicholas read mostly non-fiction as a child; he knew every country in Europe, even before knowing all fifty states, from reading World War II tomes. Nicholas still reads non-fiction, but he writes fiction. My son Timothy read so much fiction when growing up that I quickly gave up the idea of pre-reading all his books. He still suggests some of the best fiction authors I have read, such as Robert Littel and Bernard Cornwall. My son James reads biographies, and my son Nathaniel reads fantasy and sci-fi. I get excited when I have a chance to talk to my adult children about what they are reading, or when I can suggest a book that particularly fits them as an individual. Pleasure reading is an individual sport, but talking about books is a team event. It connects us to others.

After finishing a novel, I love looking at reviews on Goodreads to see what other people thought about it. I especially love that "You too? I thought I was the only one" feeling C. S. Lewis describes.[2] Every once in a while I find that I disagree with a good friend about a book. Sometimes that is a cut the friendship can't bear; but most of the time, it is okay.

Reading for pleasure is just that. It is the easiest kind of reading habit to begin, and that is exactly what it should be—a beginning. We don't end our reading habit with just those books we love, but we have to start there. As our reading muscles grow stronger, what we love will grow stronger also. If you read Victorian literature, you will find many warnings about the dangers of novel reading. Hudson Taylor's biography makes reading a novel seem like a terrible sin indeed. Why is this? I think it is because we can become lazy in what brings us pleasure. We find reading romance novels or modern novels so easy that we have a hard time enjoying something truly well-written from another era. Since the invention of the internet, I have allowed myself to be talked into reading many inferior modern novels. They are almost always a huge disappointment to me, and yet over and over again I let someone sway me into trying one. I am sad when I think of all the moms who get stuck only reading modern novels. There are only so many ways to disguise an unreliable narrator and Wilkie Collins already did it. I fear that I sound reproachful and curmudgeonly, but I have decided to go ahead and speak the truth from my perspective since that is all I really have to offer to the great conversation centered on books. We all have to start somewhere.

Murder mysteries are a great place to start reading good books because in their heyday many excellent writers wrote them. Writers like Edmund Crispin, a composer, or Michael Innes, a true

British professor, or Dorothy Sayers, a British intellectual, or P. D. James, an English civil servant—all wrote murder mysteries. While there is a place for a well-written English cozy like those by Patricia Wentworth, the more robust titles will increase our strength for weightier future reading. One other reason murder mysteries are a great place to start is that they are usually page-turners. They make the beginning stages of the habit of reading easy. Just as it is helpful for our children who are just beginning to read chapter books to run through a summer of *The Bobbsey Twins*, it is also helpful for us to run through a whole series of books by Ellis Peters or Josephine Tey as we develop the habit of reading. Finally, Dorothy Sayers says in her first Harriet Vane story *Strong Poison,* "In detective stories virtue is always triumphant. They're the purest literature we have."[3] There you have it, the definitive word on the purity of the detective novel.

A well-crafted novel is often superior to any other kind of reading, because change occurs first in our imaginations.

In order to find those moments to read, a mother must believe those moments are useful and that reading is important, even when it is enjoyable. I once read a memoir of a woman whose mother sat on the couch and smoked and read throughout the memoirist's whole childhood. She happily played on the beach while her mother sometimes got up long enough to spread peanut butter on some bread for her. Surprisingly, this writer did not grow up bitter about this lifestyle. As a member of the "oh-dear-where-has-the-time-gone-let's-eat-cereal" club, I loved that book very much.

And so reading for pleasure is not just fun, it is imperative. We must read for pleasure, or we will never develop the muscles to read more seriously.

One of the biggest hindrances to pleasure reading in the modern age is binge-watching. It is much easier to watch something than to read something. I like binge-watching as much as the next person, and if I admitted how many British police dramas I have watched, this would be obvious and embarrassing. I do have a bit of a rule in place—I don't watch until I have finished a book. I usually read throughout the week, often completing books on Sunday afternoons when I have the most uninterrupted time. This makes Sunday evenings my best binge-watching time. My husband and I loved Sunday nights with *The Durrells of Corfu* for a couple of years. Lately *All Creatures Great and Small* has captured our attention. Next stop: a Viking Cruise?

I am also usually reading several books at once. That way when I finish one, I don't have to try hard to pick up another because I already have. This plan also works well with my changing moods. Just because I don't feel like reading that Agatha Christie novel on my bedside table right now doesn't mean I don't feel like tackling that darker Susan Hill novel, or that lighter P. G. Wodehouse. Having different books for different moods helps me keep reading.

Reading for pleasure is not just a stopping place on the way to higher things. Novel reading in itself can be virtuous. I have learned more through fictional stories than from self-help books. Fictional towns can open our eyes to what community looks like, to how to treat the good among us and the bad, that what appears is not always what is, that help comes from unexpected places, that there is always hope. A well-drawn character is complex and interesting.

There is a great debate among historians on the best way to tell history. Is history a factual record of what happened when, or is it the story that matters? Can the facts sometimes skew the reality of what really happened? Can a factually incorrect story convey what really happened sometimes better? These are questions to ponder as we read novels. We should be discerning readers. Story is a powerful force, and in that way we need to enter a story alert and ready to interact with the ideas that come our way, because ideas have consequences. It is good to let stories take us sometimes to places we do not want to go for the very reason that we do not want to go there. Stories can make us aware of the dangers waiting for us in the real world. A well-crafted novel is often superior to any other kind of reading, because change occurs first in our imaginations.

Reading Non-Fiction

I have noticed that as I have grown older, my reading preferences have changed. I still love a great novel, although they are increasingly difficult to find, but when I look over my reading for a given year, the non-fiction section is increasing. Non-fiction includes all kinds of books. My favorite non-fiction categories are history and biography. Some historical accounts are more compelling than fiction. A few years ago I went down a World War I rabbit hole. Beware, that is a deep hole. I cannot find my way out of it. When I hear of a new book on the subject, I am all-in. World War I changed the course of history, and as a signpost of that change, it is a time period full of poetry—first the poetry of those clinging to the Edwardian era as it slipped away, and then the poetry of the bitter as they tried to climb out of the trenches. Most didn't make it.

After reading a few fictional books on Richard III, bless his heart, including Shakespeare's unforgettably negative portrait, I got sidetracked on him for awhile. I am not sure I could ever turn down a book about Richard III. Is he a good guy or a bad guy? I still don't know, but I did see the place in The Tower of London (not a tower, by the way), where they found the skeletons of two little boys, perhaps the little missing princes. I still tend to think that Henry VIII's desire for legitimacy drove those stories of an evil Richard, but they are certainly tenacious.

Letting ourselves go on these long rabbit trails can promote much learning. Charlotte Mason reminds us that education is the science of relations. Everything we learn connects to other things. We can find the most uncanny connections between the most diverse subjects we study. Maybe I see something in World War I that reminds me of the War of the Roses. This new information gleaned from wide reading might change the way I see the world today. It isn't alway bad to fall down the rabbit hole.

One of the criticisms of self-education is this very rabbit hole itself. The self-educated person misses things they might have learned if they had approached learning in a more orderly fashion. The self-educated person's education is haphazard. This is only true if we believe the modern construct of education. When we see that people only learn what they pay attention to, then we see that the person who is paying attention the most learns the most. You can teach students all day long in an orderly, obvious way, beginning with, "The policeman is your friend," and ending with Kant.

Very often, though, they checked out at "Snowflakes are unique." At least, they should have if they were paying attention. And, after all, even experts in their field have gaps in their overall learning.

Chesterton says it best:

> What is education? Properly speaking, there is no such thing as education. Education is simply the soul of a society as it passes from one generation to another ... What we need is to have a culture before we hand it down. In other words, it is a truth, however sad and strange, that we cannot give what we have not got, and cannot teach to other people what we do not know ourselves.[4]

Reading widely in the category of non-fiction is not only educational, it is fun. Many of the women I know who read novels, also relentlessly read along the rabbit trails of science and history those novels lead them down. My local book club has become a comedy of rabbit trails each month as we try to discuss the novel but get sidetracked by the myriads of references to other things we come across in our reading. My book club gals are downright scary in their pursuit of knowledge through rabbit trails. I believe their children will benefit from this broad accumulation of knowledge as well.

Long before we could Google (do we have a dance named that yet?), I enjoyed reading about what I was reading about. Usually when I finished a novel, I headed to the library for a biography of the author. No reading is quite so satisfying and provocative as biography. I have read biographies of almost all my favorite authors including Nathaniel Hawthorne, Dorothy Sayers, C. S. Lewis,

Beatrix Potter, Amy Carmichael, Agatha Christie, and many, many more. A good biography can stick to your bones. Often I find myself disagreeing with a biographer, which can keep me arguing in my mind with them for years. Seriously, Shakespeare was Shakespeare.

Reading Poetry

I am always sad to hear someone say they hate poetry, and I hear that frequently. I don't suppose that poetry stands a chance in these utilitarian times, and yet if we truly understood it, we would see it is the most fruitful pursuit of all. First, you need the faith to believe that it is of value. Then you need to overcome your ignorance and begin reading it. The easiest way to read poetry is out loud. It helps you feel the rhythm.

When I first began reading *The Idylls of the King* by Tennyson, it was just so-so to me. Suddenly, though, while reading it aloud, I realized that while it didn't rhyme, it did have a meter. After that, I couldn't get enough of it. I loved letting the words dance off the page. Shakespeare can be like this, as he often writes in meter when you least expect it. You might notice that the last line of the scene rhymed. It might have been a couplet. This should alert you that a good portion of the scene before was written in iambic pentameter.

> The easiest way to read poetry is out loud. It helps you feel the rhythm.

When I was seventeen years old, I accidentally discovered iambic pentameter while reading *The Taming of the Shrew*. After that, I fell in love with Shakespeare. Iambic pentameter is the same beat as your heart and mine. At the time I didn't say,

"Oh, golly, iambic pentameter." I didn't know what it was called for ages and ages, but I did "know" it, and when I found it was a thing with a name, I was delighted—or more truly, I was in love.

For some reason, in spite of my dreadful public school education, I loved poetry. It must have come through my wide reading. Everything I learned must have come through that, because I hardly know where else it could have come from. In seventh grade, I wrote pages and pages of poetry, and for some reason, the boy who sat in front of me in homeroom always asked me to read my poems and often suggested themes. I never once got the feeling he was making fun of me. In eighth grade, my English teacher asked me if she could read them, and she also encouraged me. In ninth grade, I showed them to my grandmother. Later, I found out my mother had read my poetry notebook and that was the end of that. I threw them all away. In my mind, I burned them, but I can't think of how I would have accomplished that. I am not at all sorry about this. It would be dreadful to have to read them today. Now that I know more about poetry, I am not so likely to try my hand at it. This is a little bit sad though. Sometimes it takes innocence to create, and I have lost that. Now I know Milton, and he has forever barred me from the table. But maybe that is just pride after all. Pride is what takes the place of innocence, isn't it?

Poetry is a tricky thing. One of my favorite devotionals, *Streams in the Desert,* is filled with the most awful poetry. I always have to skip the poems. It is best to start reading poetry with an anthology of the very best poetry, like a Quiller-Couch edition of *The Oxford Book of English Verse*. Just read a poem a day, out loud, to begin. Once again, the mother teaching her children has the advantage here, because she already has the structure to add in the reading of a poem. What about reading poetry at meal times? Poetry was one of the earliest things I added to Morning Time. It came on the heels of nursery rhymes, and that reminds me why I probably loved poetry from a young age. My mother read me nursery rhymes, and my grandmother did too. I can still hear my grandmother reciting—

> I am a poor peppermint stick
> All dressed in red and white,
> And when I go out for a walk
> I never come back again.

—complete with hand motions.

Rarely are nursery rhymes bad poetry.

Reading Aloud

Reading is one of those things which ebb and flow with the season of a mother's life. A mother, a person, should always be reading something, in my opinion, but how much can vary over the years. Before I had children, I read about fifty books a year. Now that most of my children are grown, I read about a hundred, but there were long stretches of time where it didn't seem like I read much at all. I had a ten-year period where I didn't read anything at all except what I read to the children. That is what saved me. I started reading aloud.

Reading aloud became my favorite activity while raising my children. I loved to read, but I wasn't getting any time to do it. I read picture books to the boys when they were little, and I enjoyed that, but it didn't satisfy the need I had for more intellectual fodder. Then, when my oldest was almost five, I picked up a few chapter books and started reading them out loud to him. He was entranced, enchanted. He could never get enough. That was a lucky break. We started reading aloud right after we read our Bible and practiced our Awana verses in the morning. In essence, WE started homeschooling. By that, I mean that we both were learning. In *Mere Motherhood*, I say you could call it kindergarten, but if it was, then I was in kindergarten too.

I had an antique book with chapters on Daniel Boone and George Washington. It is hard to remember now that when I read that book, I didn't really know anything about those men. Even a short chapter in a children's history book taught me more than I knew before. In that way my mind was fed, and that is how I continued to grow as a person after I had children. I had known when I graduated from high school that I was ignorant of so much—now I began to understand just how ignorant. Almost everything we read aloud opened my eyes to the wonders of the world and history. I was enchanted too.

We ended up spending hours and hours each day reading aloud. For the next couple of years, we would read aloud in the morning, eventually setting a structure for reading called Morning Time that I still follow today. We also read in the afternoon, during the little ones' naps, and in the evenings, when my husband Tim came home from work.

Before I'd had children, I had read Gladys Hunt's book *Honey for a Child's Heart*, a wonderful guide to choosing books for children. But now I began to pore over it for suggestions, marking up the book lists in the back of the book. Over the years, I marked the lists with all kinds of marks—RA for Read Aloud, initials for which child read which book. Before it was over, we had probably covered 80% of the lists in that book. I never found another book list quite as lovely as that one, although I now own many books about books and love them all.

Once upon a time, I was learning *about* books, and now I have *read* so many of them. Once they were new worlds to be conquered, now they are old friends to be remembered. I have always had trouble rereading since there are so many books I have yet to read, yet the nature of reading aloud meant that I did reread as more children came along. Some books I have read four or five times. Those are the kind of books that never grow old. If I reread a book, you can be sure I did it because I enjoyed it just as much as the children did and sometimes maybe more. Alex, my youngest, doesn't remember *The Little House* series because he was pretty young when I read it for the last time in our family. In some ways this shocks and even depresses me, but then I remember that I have read those books at least four times, each time as a read-aloud. Of course, I remember.

I still read aloud. Reading aloud was my preparation for so many things in life. It was a big part of my education. I even ended up having a job in which I read aloud everyday to my student. Isn't it amazing how God opens the doors he prepares us to go through? Even though I was at home for twenty-five years, teaching my children, and reading aloud, I was still being prepared for that time after they all grew up when God had other plans for me. Do not despise the years you have at home with your children. You will find that if you are faithful to use your time wisely, all those hours spent reading and learning with your children will very often make you the smartest person in the room—unless that room is filled with mothers who read aloud to their children.

Why is that? People don't read anymore. There are too many other distractions. People who do read rise to the top. Readers know stuff. Readers can intelligently talk to others from all walks of life. Reading provides a broad and liberal education, and reading aloud is the way in which mothers at home, with little time to spare, can continue their own education.

> Readers can intelligently talk to others from all walks of life.

You don't have to limit your reading aloud to novels or historical fiction, although those are excellent categories. The time spent reading novels, is time spent learning to understand other people and other worlds. It is always valuable. But you can also read aloud history books, science narratives, biographies, and travel books. AmblesideOnline[5] is a great place to find read-alouds in these other genres. As your children grow older, your choices expand. I always tried to read up to the oldest children because I knew that the younger children still gleaned from hearing harder books. But eventually, with nine children, I did have to start a separate read-aloud time for a few of the younger children right after lunch, so that I could circle back to some old favorites like *Winnie-the-Pooh* or *The Chronicles of Narnia*. But even then the older children would often chime in from the other room or wander in to listen.

In my opinion, reading aloud is the single best investment in the future a busy mother can make. It is a way to make the densest broth for future soup. It is a way to keep the mother of a large family from being in a constant state of juggling ages and grades. The more of their education that comes from reading aloud, the more time is freed up for individual pursuits. It is the easiest way to redeem the time given to you for yourself and for your children. Reading aloud is a win-win for now and for the future.

Reading the Classics

After we have flexed our reading muscles for a while and moved on from Ellis Peters to P. D. James to Dickens to Trollope, what are known as the "good books," we might be ready to tackle some of the books known as the Great Books.[6] In fact, if you have been reading aloud to your children, you have probably covered many of the books John Senior mentions in his lovely "1,000 Good Books" list. A good many of those selections are picture books, so you may be surprised and encouraged by how many of those books you have already read.

In truth, we might just want to jump in and read a Great Book even before we are ready for it, because more than likely our minds will find something to feed on there as others have before us. That is how Great Books work. There are all kinds of plans and resources to hold your hand through reading some of the Great Books. The Harvard Classics is a beautifully bound set of Great Books and Mortimer J. Adler's *Great Books of the Western World* is another. Peter Leithart has several instructional books on various classics, and The Great Courses covers most of these books in one audio course or another. Our book club used Wes Callahan to guide us through *The Aeneid*. The House of Humane Letters with Angelina Stanford and Thomas Banks offers excellent resources for reading through hard books, and *The Literary Life Podcast* also often covers classics.[7]

Or you can just pick up a Great Book and start reading. Often that is the best way since it is the easiest. If you need help, you can go looking for it then. I try to always have some Great Book in the queue. One year I finally read *The Aeneid*. Last year I read Boswell's *Life of Johnson,* and this year I finished *The Canterbury Tales*. My usual pattern when reading a Great Book is to listen on audio just to get me going and then read it after that in print. Reading aloud is also a great way to enjoy most of these books, as many of them were made to be performed out loud. If you don't have any family members to read out loud to, try finding a private place to read out loud to yourself. Talk about self-care!

I have not been able to read any classic in its original language unless it was written in English. I once had a book clerk laugh out loud at me when I asked for a copy of *Pilgrim's Progress* in its original language. He replied with a rude guffaw, "In English?" Of course, what I meant was that I didn't want a paraphrase or abridgment. But I did learn something that day. Be careful how you say things. At least, I started to learn that. I tend to be careless with words. But in spite of that, I still find it beautiful to listen to others read the *Iliad* aloud in Greek even when I don't understand a word of it.

At this point in my life, it doesn't look like I will read all of the Great Books. But I intend to keep reading and rereading as many as I can until I am no longer able.

Christians are Bible readers and as such are already well-versed in reading ancient literature. If we have read the King James version, we are well on our way to enjoying Shakespeare unimpeded. Dryden's version of Plutarch is not that different from the good old King James, and while Plutarch is challenging on any day of the week, it is less challenging to those accustomed to Elizabethan sentence structure. The easiest way to prepare ourselves and our children for a Great Books education is to begin by reading the KJV out loud as a family.

The Bible is the *logos* that prepares us to meet words and understand them. As C. S. Lewis says, "It is a good rule, after reading a new book, never to allow yourself another new one till you have read an old one in between."[8] This is a good rule for many reasons, most especially because we are drowning in the words of modernity or post-modernity. More than at any other time in the history of the world, we are immersed in our own thoughts and our own times. This deluge of modern words apparently leaves us unable to understand past ideas and past ways of expression. While we preach tolerance, we are singularly untalented at tolerating the past or understanding it. Maybe we need to heed Lewis's words by reading more than one old book for every new one we read.

The Book Collector

Most readers I have known over the years eventually become infected with a disease known as book buying. The Erasmus quote, "When I have a little money, I buy books; and if I have any left, I buy food and clothes," is not a joke—it is a way of life.[9] In my book *Mere Motherhood,* I mentioned this book-buying addiction, and a lady contacted me about it. She felt that I was encouraging addiction. She had been an addict of some sort, and she recognized that I was also an addict. *Touché.* In the spirit of fair play, let me say right up front that while I like to joke about buying too many books, and I have indeed often spent money I should not have on books, and while I do encourage others to buy books, addiction is bad. I do know people who buy books and do not read books. I spent many years collecting books which I eventually sold or recognized as inferior. My library has diminished over the years from possibly 6,000 volumes or more to probably 600 books. Many of those books I passed along to my own children, and some I sold to other homeschoolers. Some went in the garbage, and some were sold at a secondhand shop. There was a time and a place in my life for a huge library and a time and a place for a smaller library. I still buy books, but I am much more careful these days. Sometimes, though, I find that I need a volume that I got rid of and then I am sad indeed.

Recently, my son and his family moved back east. When I visited them, I not only saw my dear grandchildren but also many of my old friends among his bookshelves. It reminded me that it was good to give my books away.

Book buying, though, is a delightful hobby for readers. Getting to know the very best books and buying them is richly satisfying. The best book collecting experiences for me came in the early years. I pored over *Honey for a Child's Heart* day after day. One day, when our oldest was around five, we heard the library was having a book sale. I loaded up the kids in the car with a wagon, and we headed to the book sale. We bought hundreds of books over the few days that first sale lasted, and my two oldest boys started to get a feel for what was a good book. My husband got busy finding or building bookshelves. The more I learned about books, the more fun going to used book sales was and is. Finding a rare copy of *My Book House* or Hillyer's *A Child's History of the World* is intoxicating (addict alert). Even though my library is small now, I still can't resist the occasional book sale. Recently, while waiting for a rain delay at an away baseball game, my husband and I saw a sign for a book sale. We had the best time during that severe thunderstorm perusing books. I was able to buy a small set of Harvard Classics deluxe editions for our son Andrew who had just moved into his first house. He had been about to buy a set for over $300, and I bought this one for less than $20. What better housewarming gift could I have found? And what better affirmation of the bookish life than to have a son who wanted them?

Many older homeschooling moms are opening up their home libraries as lending libraries to the broader community. I have at least two friends who are doing this. While I passed my library on to the next generation, these ladies have preserved their libraries intact for lending out to other families. This is a huge service to the community, because many public libraries have sold or gotten rid of the very best volumes to make room for the most inane modern fodder. I am sad to say that I have found real treasures dumpster diving at local public school libraries. I don't randomly dumpster dive, but alerts sometimes go out from sad librarians for homeschoolers to come rescue books. Rescuing books is rescuing culture.

Across the street from me lives a lovely homeschooling family who also go to my church. One day, Rachel texted me that she was selling some furniture to buy more books. While I do not want to encourage young moms to spend too much money on books, I can't help but feel that their lives will be enriched. When Rachel runs out of money, she will still be able to borrow books from me, but even more from my friend Jeannette Tulis who possibly owns 10,000 books and freely lends them out to families. In my church alone, at least three older homeschooling moms are nationally known experts on books, and my church doesn't overtly promote homeschooling. Many moms in our church probably don't realize the treasure trove of wisdom sitting quietly in our pews. Wisdom that is backed up by hundreds of volumes of books and hours of reading.

Book collecting is a noble hobby which should go hand-in-hand with book reading. Like any hobby, it can overrun and overturn your life. We are creatures of extremes, but just because it can get out of control doesn't mean it has to. We can trust God for those heady moments when we run across a book sale and find a treasure or two. The serendipity of it is part of the fun.

Book Clubs

Several years ago, a group of young moms I know started a book club. We met at the park to decide on our selections. We wanted to read liberally across the classics with a few lighter choices to keep us from going insane. We have the most fun meeting at a park to pick out our selections for each semester. We began with *The Abolition of Man* by C. S. Lewis. A couple days before our meeting, Michael Ward came to Chattanooga to discuss this very work. It was like having C. S. Lewis himself. Michael is an Oxford man who regularly visits The Eagle and The Child, the pub where the Inklings met in Oxford. I love happy accidents. *The Abolition of Man* was not an easy read for our group, although it was short. Many of our selections have been challenging. Our second book was a novel which I picked titled *A Lantern in her Hand,* by Bess Streeter Aldrich. I picked it because one of my all-time favorite books on motherhood is Aldrich's second volume, *A White Bird Flying.* I tried to encourage the girls to read the second book even if they didn't like the first one, as some didn't. I was happy to hear later that they did enjoy *A White Bird Flying,* a book I compare to *Hannah Coulter.* Our third book was *Come Be My Light,* by Mother Theresa, a series of letters she wrote over the years about her prolonged "dark night of the soul." I was dreading our book discussion because many girls had already told me they didn't like the book at all, and I also didn't love it. We all learned something interesting the night of our club. Discussions about books you don't like can be more interesting than discussions about books you do like. We had a lively and fun discussion on deep theological matters that night. A book club is a great place to learn how to disagree politely and not to be afraid of disagreement. We can choose not to be threatened by someone else's ideas even while choosing to disagree.

Our book club is structured for only twelve members. The original six girls each invited one other member. When someone drops out, then we meet to invite someone new, never adding more than twelve. Most meetings have around six to ten attendees. It's not that easy for moms to get away consistently, and we already have had three new babies born to club members. But six to ten is plenty for a good discussion. We have a mix of younger moms and older moms. This is a must for the best discussion across the generations. Not only so older moms can share their wisdom, but so that the younger moms can also help the older moms understand a newer generation.

We start each meeting with prayer and poetry and end it with Scripture reading. Different members take turns hosting, and each month different girls pick out the poetry and Scripture. But honestly, I think a book club with opening prayer and discussion would be perfect. Sometimes we can bog things down with too many good things.

When I see the joy and camaraderie in our group, I can imagine it lasting for the next twenty years, organically moving and changing as the members change. I hope in twenty years I will still be a part of this book club.

A Woman I Know: Bonnie Buckingham

Many early homeschooling moms stood in the middle of changing worlds. As the libraries adapted to those changes, these moms were situated to buy excellent books at low prices. In that way, many women accumulated wonderful libraries and much wisdom. On a recent trip to North Carolina, I stayed in the home of one of the best of these women, Bonnie Buckingham. When you walk in the doors of her spacious home, you might as well be walking into a Hobbit hole for all the cozy charm. Bookshelves, large and small, adorn ALL of her many rooms, along with tea cups, linens, lace, interesting lamps and beautiful prints. While many of her books are scattered throughout the house (I found it hard to sleep in a bedroom with so many treasures!), she has a special place tucked away in her basement which is a real lending library. Here she catalogs thousands of books and lends them out to the larger community. The kind of knowledge of books she carries in her head is inspiring. It is the result of a lifetime pursuit of knowledge. You cannot call it a hobby because her faithfulness to pursue books and knowledge has produced rare fruit. Her knowledge of art, literature, history, and poetry make her an ideal travel companion as I found on my trip to England's Lake District. Walking the hills in the Lake District with Bonnie and her delightful husband Ken made me feel a little like C. S. Lewis on a walking tour with his pals, especially when they bought me a nice Lake District pale ale at the end of the day.

Back at home, her lovely house is a haven of hospitality. She does not keep her purchases at bay from visitors. Although all her children are grown, she continues to pour back into the community, teaching humanities classes in her home, classes I would love to attend. Her meals are infused with the kind of conversation one selfishly longs for more often.

Young homeschooling mom, this is who you can be someday!

The Ideal and the Reality

It is difficult to imagine while mired in a life filled with children bickering and dirty laundry that it could become something bearing such rich fruit, but faithfulness in the little things, and with the little people does bear fruit. The best fruit comes after the longest wait. I was far into my forties before I read the *Iliad*. I never even got around to reading it with my older children, although I did assign it. When I did finally read it aloud to my youngest two children, I realized that it was better that way. We all remember those out-loud readings better. Epics are usually meant to be read that way. Even at my age, there are many classics I have yet to read. I don't want to just frantically check off books, and I don't have to.

The habit of reading can be just a tiny faithful decision made each day. Five or ten minutes can turn into thirty or forty until maybe you do just need to make sure that dinner hasn't burned or, as was more likely with me, isn't still in the freezer.

More recently, a boy I was teaching expressed discouragement in reading *Caddie Woodlawn*. I knew it was easier than he imagined, but I decided to do an experiment to show him. I asked him to read a chapter while I timed him. Being a boy, he was all over that! It took him less than five minutes. The book seemed daunting to him until I showed him how little time it took to read a chapter. Five minutes a day for 180 days a year is 180 chapters. If a book has on average eighteen chapters, that is ten books a year or 120 books in twelve years of school. What if you read ten minutes a day? You don't have to read 120 books today. Try reading for five minutes and watch the years roll by.

What if you read ten minutes a day?

Maybe it is just the kind of people I like to read about, but I can hardly remember reading a biography that is not about a reader. As I write this, I am reading about Annie Dillard in *An American Childhood*, Elizabeth Goudge in her memoir *The Joy of Snow*, a gift from another bookish friend, and Madeleine L'Engle in her *Crosswick Journals* memoir series. All of these books are haunted by other books. Some of these book suggestions go onto the frustratingly long to-be-read list; others are old friends. It is delightful to come across a reference to an old book in another book.

"You too? I thought I was the only one."

Suggested Reading

Favorite Mystery Writers

P. D. James	Ngaio March
Dorothy Sayers	Agatha Christie
Edmund Crispin	Bruce Alexander
Michael Innes	Susan Hill
Ellis Peters	Charles Todd
Josephine Tey	Anthony Horowitz
Sally Wright	Peter Grainger

Other Favorite Fiction Authors

Helen MacInnes	Elizabeth Goudge
Tim Powers	George MacDonald
Olive Ann Burns	Connie Willis
Caroline Gordon	Walter Scott

Series of Books to Get You Reading

1. *The Chronicles of Brother Cadfael* series by Ellis Peters
2. Fairacre series or Thrush Green series by Miss Read
3. Lord Peter Wimsey books by Dorothy L. Sayers
4. Mr. Mulliner, Jeeves and Wooster, or Smith books by P. G. Wodehouse
5. *The Mitford Years* series by Jan Karon

Books about Books

1. *Honey for a Child's Heart* by Gladys Hunt
2. *Invitation to the Classics* by Cowan and Guinness

3. *Used and Rare* by Lawrence and Nancy Goldstone (and others by the authors)
4. *Howard's End is on the Landing* by Susan Hill
5. *The Joy of Reading* by Charles Van Doren
6. *Children and Books* by May Hill Arbuthnot
7. *A Bequest of Wings* by Annis Duff
8. *An Experiment in Criticism* by C. S. Lewis
9. *Bandersnatch* by Diana Pavlac Glyer
10. *Jacob's Room is Full of Books* by Susan Hill

Ten Favorite Fiction Books

1. *Possession* by A. S. Byatt
2. *The Name of the Rose* by Umberto Eco
3. *To Say Nothing of the Dog* by Connie Willis
4. *Life After Life* by Kate Atkinson
5. *A Lantern in Her Hand* by Bess Streeter Aldrich
6. *Jayber Crow* by Wendell Berry
7. *In This House of Brede* by Rumer Godden
8. *The Enchanted April* by Elizabeth von Arnim
9. *That Hideous Strength* by C. S. Lewis
10. *Reunion* by Fred Uhlman

Ten Favorite Non-Fiction Books

1. *In Search of the Source* by Neil Anderson
2. *The Hiding Place* by Corrie Ten Boom
3. *A Man Called Peter* by Catherine Marshall
4. *The Birth of the Modern* by Paul Johnson
5. *A Distant Mirror* by Barbara Tuchman

6. *From Dawn to Decadence* by Jacques Barzun
7. *The Company They Keep* by Diana Pavlov Glyer
8. *A Preface to Paradise Lost* by C. S. Lewis
9. *The Art of the Commonplace* by Wendell Berry
10. *The Mind of the Maker* by Dorothy L. Sayers

Ten Poetry Books

1. *The Oxford Book of English Verse* edited by Arthur Quiller-Couch
2. *How Does a Poem Mean* by John Ciardi
3. *The Classic Hundred Poems* edited by William Harmon
4. *Rules for the Dance* by Mary Oliver
5. *Storytelling and Other Poems*, Childcraft, vol. 2 (1954)
6. *The Idylls of the King* by Alfred, Lord Tennyson
7. *The Poet's Corner* by John Lithgow
8. *You Come Too: Favorite Poems for Young Readers* by Robert Frost
9. A collection of Shakespeare's sonnets
10. *101 Famous Poems* edited by Roy Cook

Ten Biographies

1. *The Inklings* by Humphrey Carpenter
2. *Beatrix Potter: A Life in Nature* by Linda Lear
3. *Surprised by Joy* by C. S. Lewis
4. *Agatha Christie: An Elusive Woman* by Lucy Worsley
5. *The Story of Charlotte Mason* by Essex Cholmondeley
6. *My Early Life: 1874-1904* by Winston Churchill

7. The *Crosswick Journals* series by Madeleine L'Engle
8. *The Narnian* by Alan Jacobs
9. *A Chance to Die: The Life and Legacy of Amy Carmichael* by Elisabeth Elliot
10. *Up from Slavery* by Booker T. Washington

Ten Great Books for Beginners

1. The *Iliad* by Homer
2. The *Odyssey* by Homer
3. The *Aeneid* by Virgil
4. The *Phaedrus* by Plato
5. The *Divine Comedy* by Dante
6. *Paradise Lost* by Milton
7. Plutarch's *Lives of the Noble Greeks and Romans*
8. *The Canterbury Tales* by Geoffrey Chaucer
9. *War and Peace* by Leo Tolstoy
10. The Complete Works of William Shakespeare

Ten Favorite Classic Novels

1. *Middlemarch* by George Elliot
2. *Pride and Prejudice* by Jane Austen
3. *Ivanhoe* by Walter Scott
4. *David Copperfield* by Charles Dickens
5. *The Moonstone* by Wilkie Collins
6. *A Tale of Two Cities* by Charles Dickens
7. *The Vicar of Wakefield* by Oliver Goldsmith
8. *Bleak House* by Charles Dickens
9. *Barchester Towers* by Anthony Trollope
10. *Vanity Fair* by William Makepeace Thackeray

Growth Ideas

- Google the "1,000 Good Books" list and check off the ones you have already read!
- Find a murder mystery author and read through their whole catalog.
- Join a book club or start one!
- Find someone to read aloud to, an older person or a younger one, or one far away. You can record chapters.

CHAPTER FOUR

The Natural Mother

> Even if I knew that tomorrow the world would go to
> pieces, I would still plant my apple tree.
>
> Martin Luther

Nature Study

The natural mother. By this I do not mean the organic mother who feeds her family expensive foods, nor the non-chemical mother who slathers coconut oil on her face (as I do), but rather the mother who wants to learn about the outdoors by *being* outdoors. The outdoors is the most wonderful place to develop the habit of attention, perhaps the most important habit of all, at least in regards to education. In her first book, *Home Education*, Charlotte Mason says:

> Consider, too, what an unequaled mental train-
> ing the child-naturalist is getting for any study or
> calling under the sun—the powers of attention,
> of discrimination, of patient pursuit, growing
> with the growth, what will they not fit him for?[1]

Or what will they not fit us grown-ups for too? Perhaps because the out-of-doors, as the old-timers like to call it, is less tame than the indoors, there is a certain mystery and danger that lurks outdoors. There is a sense of adventure too, because as Bilbo says, "It's a dangerous business, Frodo, going out your door . . .You step into the Road, and if you don't keep your feet, there is no knowing where you might be swept off to."[2] I have often been tempted since childhood to follow some path on and on and on. When I was a young girl, it was the stream in the woods behind my grandparents' house. Where was it going? Where would it lead? I was too much of a rule-follower to ever find out, but I still wonder.

You must make yourself walk out the door with your children.

Playing in that copse year after year as a child filled me with enough wonder to last a lifetime. It was my own hundred-acre wood. I could walk its paths even now in my mind. I was devastated when they tore it down and put in a subdivision. I remember those newer, bigger houses at the end of my grandparents' street as if they were palaces of gold, and yet today they have become worn and dingy, out-of-style, not holding up to the promises they made. The woods made no promises. The woods were unknowns. I remember them well.

I have always been an outdoor girl—and I have the melanoma to prove it—but I still can't bring myself to hide from the sun. My mother insisted her children play outside, and she practices what she preached even today. Every day she takes several walks outside—rain or snow. I used to find this annoying. She would visit me, and I would be in the middle of laundry or cooking, and she would want to take a walk. Perhaps it was the hint that "I needed it" that bothered me. It is hard for a young mother to listen to her mother. But now that I am older, I am not so threatened by her walks and try to emulate her example. In fact, lately you will find me walking with my mother *and* my daughter. That is exceedingly abundant!

The importance of nature study in a technological age is exponentially increased, in my opinion. We are desperately in need of understanding the world outside of our devices. We are being swallowed up in virtual reality while forgetting those things our ancestors have tried to pass on to us about the real world, the natural world. In his book on nature study, *The Lost Art of Reading Nature's Signs*, Tristan Gooley makes the point that nature is rarely random. That is the mystery! That tree curls oddly for a reason, a reason you can figure out! All of nature is mysterious, but that mystery is something we can learn. If reading murder mysteries is fun and satisfying, it is because the universe is a mystery to solve. We may not be able to figure out the genome sequence all by ourselves, but this very day we can go outside and look for patterns.

You are four chapters into this book, so this is not going to be a surprise, but the first step in knowing nature is to *go outside*. Sit on your front stoop if that is all you can do. Sit on your balcony or porch. Just go outside and notice things. If you want to really, really notice things, pick up a notebook and write something about what you see from that same spot every single day for a year. That is nature study.

Gooley talks about using our own senses and drawings rather than tools which can become crutches in nature.

> You can either spend a lot of time living in remote areas without any technology, maps or compasses, or you can take the time to sketch a couple of landscapes. Only one of these is a particularly practical solution. The quality of your artwork is not important; what's vital is practicing the art of seeing and noticing.[3]

I mentioned in the chapter on reading how often people worthy of biographies are readers; they are almost equally people who sketch or draw. More on that later.

Ideally, a family should be taking a nature walk weekly. I liked to plan a whole day a week for this, because it often got pushed aside. Maybe you hope to hike weekly, and you do this for a month or so, and then life happens, as I promise it will. You don't hike for several weeks, and now a hike seems overwhelming. You think you cannot possibly skip Latin to go on a hike. Yes, you can. You can and you must. You must make yourself walk out the door with your children. Hike your neighborhood, hike your backyard, or drive to a park, but *you must do this*. Do not make a large production out of this at first. Forget the nature notebooks, the bug spray, the portable stools, the walking sticks, and the snacks. Everyone grab a water bottle and head out the door *right now*. Get that first hike under your belt. Then, next time you can add snacks for a longer hike or colored pencils for nature note-booking. The important thing, the thing itself, is the hike. Our plans often sabotage our accomplishments. The more you get outside, the more you will want to be there, and the more you will begin to see. Seeing then becomes knowing.

I am not an expert on nature notebooks, but I keep one.

I mentioned earlier that the habit of attention is the key to prayer. Seeing and paying attention to the world around us also turns us toward the Creator and prayer. I recently noticed how rarely I looked at the moon. I live in a wooded area and often don't see the moon in the evening. Sometimes, though, I see it in the early morning. One particular day, I was driving up over our ridge feeling downhearted. As I looked on the horizon, I could see a huge orange moon rising up over the Tennessee River highlighting the mountains. It was a gift from God, and it felt very personal. I started trying to pay attention to the moon more. After all, "Cynthia" means "moon goddess." I noticed that it wasn't as easy as it seemed to see the moon. Not long after this, I told the story of my big, glorious moon to a group of ladies in Colorado, and I became obsessed with catching another glimpse of the moon. Day after day went by, but I would forget to look—or when I did look, it was cloudy, or I could not find it from my porch. Some nights I went outside when I woke up after midnight to see if I could see it. I began to get paranoid. Was God withholding the moon from me? This went on for several weeks.

Then, I got the terrible phone call I was dreading: my dad was being placed in hospice care with only hours to live. We went to stay with him in the lovely hospice house in Richmond, Kentucky. For several nights, I stayed by my dad's side waking often in the middle of the night. One early morning, I walked outside the French doors of his room onto the patio which opened to a lawn and then a farmer's field. Suddenly, I realized that a huge moon was blazing before me. As I stood and stared, I became aware that the field was twinkling. Twinkling with what seemed millions of fireflies. There was the moon I had so longed to behold, and there was something else so inexplicable I would never even have asked to behold it. In one of the darkest times of my life, light was shining in the dead of midnight. Light upon light upon light. I thought then about all those failed weeks of trying to see the moon. It didn't seem to me that God had been withholding it—rather, He had been preparing my heart to see this glorious display. I recently read a passage from Thomas Merton that reminds me that God does not speak this way to me alone.

> I came up here from the monastery last night, sloshing through the cornfield, said Vespers, and put some oatmeal on the Coleman stove for supper. It boiled over while I was listening to the rain and toasting a piece of bread at the log fire. The night became very dark. The rain surrounded the whole cabin with its enormous virginal myth, a whole world of meaning, of secrecy, of silence, of rumor. Think of it: all that speech pouring down, selling nothing, judging nobody, drenching the thick mulch of dead leaves, soaking the trees, filling the gullies and crannies of the wood with water, washing out the places where men have stripped the hillside! What a thing it is to sit absolutely alone, in the forest, at night, cherished by this wonderful, unintelligible, perfectly innocent speech, the most comforting speech in the world, the talk that rain makes by itself all over the ridges, and the talk of the watercourses everywhere in the hollows! Nobody started it, nobody is going to stop it. It will talk as long as it wants, this rain. As long as it talks I am going to listen.[4]

Why should we study nature? So that we can see it and by seeing it, we will see God. Why should we get our children outside? So that we can stop preaching empty words filled with fear, and we can let them behold that all is well. Something greater than Adam is here. God is speaking to us in nature. As long as He is talking, we should listen.

Nature Walks and Nature Notebooks

Nature walks and nature notebooks go hand in hand—one is relatively simple, but one causes all kinds of confusion and angst. It is pretty simple to walk out your front door. Immediately, you are confronted with fresh air. God made that. It is natural. If we think about it, even our houses are filled with oxygen, nature. How would you draw that? I bet if you thought about it, your mind would come up with all kinds of creative ways to embody air. Herein lies the beauty of the nature notebook. It makes us think about what we see or don't see, which is often just as important. Why aren't there any birds here? Maybe I shouldn't be here either! We don't have to manufacture these sorts of questions when we draw nature. The drawing produces the questions.

Nature walks can be simple walks around the block, or they can be elaborate hikes in the mountains. I can do both of those things in the next ten minutes from my house, but now I am bragging. The first step towards easy nature hikes is move to Tennessee. The only trouble with that is ennui. Even in Tennessee inertia works against us. But our nature walks should be a combination of daily going outside our home with our eyes and ears open and planning more elaborate hikes. As I write, one of my sons is hiking a section of the Appalachian trail. He didn't invite me, and that is fine since he wouldn't even take all the snacks I offered him. He is sticking to military-style MREs (meals-ready-to-eat). I am not planning on eating those ever!

When my children were home, we got outside more than most people, but then we didn't ever take as many real hikes as I imagined. Still, we got in a fair share of good hikes, even when I was completely out of shape. The key to hiking when you are out of shape is to go in cool weather and walk slowly. Let the others run back and forth to check on you. If you plan a few excellent hikes over the school year maybe you will get one or two in. The more hikes you can take the better, even up to one a week, leaving four days for formal learning.

I don't have children who can hike with me as much now. I do like to take my grandchildren on nature walks when they visit though. I visualize myself as a hiker, and yet I have the worst time making myself hike alone or planning hikes. Thankfully, this problem has been solved for me by younger moms who invite old homeschool moms to hike with their weekly group. At least three older ladies have joined them periodically, including my good friend Jeannette, whom you will hear about later. Jeannette is invited for her extensive knowledge of flora and fauna, some of which I knew and have forgotten. Walking with these young families and Jeannette is a great refresher course for me. If you do have a nature walking group, don't forget to invite older moms or single ladies. Starting a nature group is one of the easiest ways to deal with inertia. Find a mom good at planning, and let her energy pull the rest of you along. Simply putting a date on the calendar goes a long way in overcoming ennui.

I am not an expert on nature notebooks, but I keep one. I have never been a good artist or someone who could draw; even my handwriting is shaky. I never took the time to start my own nature notebook when my children were young because I didn't have the confidence. Now that I have one, I see that confidence comes with practice. I made that age-old mistake of thinking I couldn't do something unless I was already good at it. My nature notebook is still not beautiful; it will never be *ooh*ed and *aah*ed over, but I did manage to paint a cedar waxwing for which my students extensively praised me. With no talent at all, I learned to paint a beautiful bird just by using my eyes. Sadly, I got such an extensive look at the bird because it ran into our window and died. It was such a lovely little thing and a rare bird sighting for our family. I am glad I was able to preserve its beauty in watercolors.

Nature notebooking starts with your eyes, a blank piece of paper, and a good pencil, pen, or watercolor brush with paints. The most important thing to have is your eyes. Your other senses are important too. They can alert your eyes to look. Today I decided to open the curtain in front of me as I wrote. I kept seeing debris fall from the tree right outside the window. When I took a break, I looked out the window for three or four minutes trying to figure out what was causing the continuous fall of bark and leaves. I assumed it was squirrels playing in the branches. Eventually, I pinpointed a sound coming from the tree, but I had to go outside on the deck to investigate further. After positioning myself several different ways, I finally saw a woodpecker pecking away at a dead branch at the top of the tree. I always thought of woodpeckers as quickly boring a hole and then moving along. This guy had been at the same spot for at least fifteen minutes. The bugs he must have found! I would not have been surprised if the whole branch had fallen to the ground. This got me thinking about the role of woodpeckers in the ecosystem. I knew they helped control insects, but I never thought about how they helped remove dead branches. So much to think about just because I opened the window.

We have a tendency to buy our way into a hobby. We want to take a nature walk, so we get on Amazon and read reviews of hiking boots and books. We search for the best water bottle or CamelBak. We look for walking sticks and comfortable socks. When we do this, we are getting the (Amazon) cart before the horse. Maybe your oldest pair of tennis shoes will work well on a hike. Did you know that Grandma Gatewood, who walked the entire Appalachian trail in the 1950s while in her sixties, wore canvas sneakers? I have taken more than one hike in flip-flops, usually regretting it, but I do so hate to wear shoes. Don't get sidetracked by making a hobby of searching for hiking paraphernalia instead of actually hiking. Get out and hike, and then you will see what you need. Pull out a notebook and try your hand at nature notebooking before investing in too many supplies. You don't need money to take a walk in the woods.

Naming Things: Wildflower, Herbs, Trees, etc.

Once we get good at just getting outside and seeing, we will naturally want to start knowing the names of things. Today I need to find out if what I saw was a red-headed woodpecker or a flicker. All I have to do is ask my husband, Tim. He loves birds. He has feeders all over our property feeding both birds *and* vermin. (Do I sound bitter?) But he does know the names of all the birds I will ever see.

Naming nature is one of the most satisfying ways to accumulate knowledge. To know the name of what you see is empowering. Our deep ignorance, in modern times, of the names of birds, trees, flowers, herbs, grasses, shells, animals, and all manner of flora and fauna is a sign of darkness in our souls. Even sadder than not knowing is not caring. I heard the author of *The Last Child in the Woods*, Richard Louv, remark in a speech that he believed all the emphasis on ecology and saving the planet has made a generation of children fearful of the outdoors, afraid they will cause it harm. I love reading Wendell Berry on

> Even sadder than not knowing is not caring.

these things because he manages to promote ecology and economy at the same time. Learning the name of something is the beginning of caring, and Charlotte Mason says that the end of our education should be that we care. The older I get the less I apply only to children what Charlotte Mason said. Persons. We are all persons. Persons are healthiest when they care.

I am not good anymore at names. I forget the names of people I just met, and worse, I forget the names of old friends. This is a natural part of the aging process. I don't feel too old until I am grasping for the name of that person I have known for twenty years. I love talking to "old" friends now because all the proper nouns are so hard to find in my head, but with an old friend vague sentences still connect. "Remember that, you know, thing we did with what's-her-name at the place. What a fun day we had there!" And she nods and agrees and knows exactly what I am talking about.

There is a sad day coming in my near future when I will go to visit my mother, and she will not know who I am. The Bible says,

"When my father and my mother forsake me, then the Lord will take me up."[5] I have never thought about that verse in this new light, but I think it applies. Even my mother and father, the people who named me, will forsake me by forgetting. Forgetting who I am. Who am I when I am a daughter to people who do not know me? This thought terrifies me. I do not want to face that day, but already I have seen more than a few glimpses that it is coming.

When we name things we are remembering. Remembering is one of the most important things we can do for our present and our future. Remembering is not looking back only, it is carrying those things past into the future for the preservation of culture. Charlotte Mason says about children:

> There is no knowledge so appropriate to the early
> years of a child as that of the name and look and
> behavior *in situ* of every natural object he can get
> at. "He hath so done His marvelous works that
> they ought to be had in remembrance."[6]

Some novels are good at helping us to see what this looks like. I think *The Lord of the Rings* is especially poignant in its use of names. Of course, Tolkien was a philologist. A popular online encyclopedia says that "philology is the study of language in oral and written historical sources; it is a combination of literary criticism, history, and linguistics."[7]

Words come to us with a DNA. They are full of connotation and denotation. Some names immediately tell us what we need to know. The plant bladderwort is shaped like, well, a bladder. In old herbal lore, people thought the shape of the plant was a hint to what it treated. For instance, bladderwort would be good for bladder infections according to old lore. Being alert to nuances makes naming things mysterious and fun. Can you guess what a lady's slipper looks like? I bet if you saw one you would immediately realize its name, but around here if you see one you are blessed indeed.

The easiest way to learn names is through field guides, but that can be overwhelming. I do suggest that you have field guides on hand at home for reference. Looking through a field guide just for fun can make you aware of what to look for while out of doors. These days you can use your phone to take pictures of rare finds and then post them on local nature groups. I belong to a Tennessee naturalist Facebook group, and the collective knowledge of that group almost makes wasting time on Facebook profitable. Once, in Alabama, I carried two wildflower field guides in my pockets on a hike—the hike where I fell into the stream.

Maybe today you will identify trees and next week you will bring along a wildflower book.

I recommend only taking one field guide with you at a time. Maybe today you will identify trees and next week you will bring along a wildflower book. Consider the season. Wildflowers abound in early spring. It is often easier to identify tree bark in the winter and tree foliage in the summer. Migratory birds can be found in early spring or autumn. This is the time to see birds you won't see on a regular basis. Walking with a knowledgeable person is almost better than a field guide. Be alert to how they use their field guides.

Sometimes searching for the name of something can be frustrating. It seems like it should be easy, but then you find a million things it could be. Learning the names of things is not a quick trick. It is a slow process. Often we have to see something over and over again before we remember the name. The more you go outside with your eyes open, the quicker these things will stick.

Reading about Nature

A few years ago, I read a book about a man walking the Appalachian Trail, otherwise known as "the AT," after his wife died. It was titled *Hiking Through: Finding Peace and Freedom on the Appalachian Trail* by Paul V. Stutzman. This book, for whatever reason, captured my imagination. I think it was because Paul was such an ordinary guy, not some ultra-athlete. His book led me down an AT literary trail. My next favorite book was about Grandma Gatewood, a mother of 11 children, who walked the entire trail after telling her grown children she was going for a walk. She carried a tarp and wore old-fashioned Keds, buying new pairs here and there along the way. Once again, I was inspired. Maybe I could do that? I talked to one of my sons who asked me a few probing questions that discouraged me, like "Have you thought about going to the bathroom?" But I kept reading, even rereading Bill Bryson's hilarious account of his attempt, *A Walk in the Woods*. I read so many books I felt like I had a new hobby: reading about walking. By the time I read my seventh volume on the subject, I was pretty much cured of my desire to hike the trail. Gary Sizer's *Where's the Next Shelter* was so realistic with weird toilet experiences, lost toe nails, Lyme disease, and other trail ailments, I decided that maybe C. S. Lewis-style pub crawl nature walks was more my style. Next stop England.

A Woman I Know: Jeannette Tulis

While I could have mentioned my friend Jeannette Tulis as the woman I know in the previous chapter because of her extensive home library, I decided to save her for this chapter. Jeannette is a treasure trove of nature lore. Having raised her family in the Chattanooga area, and being a Charlotte Mason purist in the truest sense, Jeannette has spent many days attending hikes and walks led by experts in the fields of flora and fauna. She not only knows when these events will take place, she herself is a handy person to have along on a hike—that is, if you are willing to slow down and linger over the plants along the way. I am usually the mom waddling ahead to make sure none of the children fall off the cliff. Jeannette arrives at any destination prepared to learn. She taught me about walking sticks and little hiking stools and which watercolors traveled in a backpack well. She does so much research on all these topics, I never have to open a browser, following the rabbit trails of reviews to choose a product. She has done the work for me. I just say, "Which shoe is best for walking the Lake District?" And she knows! I do not even have to double check. She doesn't just know because she has done the research online, she knows because she has a vast army of knowledgeable contacts for almost every nature scenario. She knows people. On any given walk, she will pull out just the right field guide for what we are staring at, and if we cannot identify it, she will relentlessly research it when she arrives home.

Jeannette's nature notebooks are beautiful. She works hard to be precise in her drawings and correct in her labeling. She rarely hikes without her nature notebook, while I like to do most of my drawing and painting at home. It was Jeannette who encouraged me to start my own nature notebook even though I had failed to do so during the years my children were at home.

One of the interesting things about homeschooling is seeing what your children do when they grow up. Younger moms like to think they can imitate other people's lives and get the same result, but after you graduate a few children you realize that children are individuals, no matter how they were raised. Jeannette's daughter Abigail grew up to be a classical artist in New York City. Her work is stunning. Jeannette's sons have excelled in scientific and technological fields. You just never know what the mind will do as a result of what it is nourished with. We are not outcome-based educators. Jeannette's children are not the *product* of her homeschool. They are individuals with their own passions and interests, just like Jeannette. The experiences she gave them by her own example nourished their minds.

> . . . after you graduate a few children you realize that children are individuals, no matter how they were raised.

Last night I attended a meeting of the C. S. Lewis Society of Chattanooga with Jeannette. The speaker was discussing *That Hideous Strength*. Jeannette sat down with several people to pick their brains about the book, which she was reading for the first time. She wanted to understand it, and she doggedly pursued that understanding by asking questions.

Jeannette is a beautiful example of a mother of passion who seeks beautiful things relentlessly.

The Ideal and the Reality

Jeannette's dogged determination can be intimidating. I am nothing at all like her, although I deeply admire her. Here is a hint to obtaining the ideal while living in the reality. Latch on to somebody who is already doing the work and glean from their fields. I say that tongue-in-cheek, but really it is true. Half the battle is knowing whom to ask or whom to hang with. If you have a friend like Jeannette, follow her around and see how much you pick up.

One year a lady asked me to bring our family nature notebooks to a conference so she could get a picture in her mind of what I was talking about. As I searched through bins and boxes and shelves, I could not find the nicer nature notebooks—those done by the more talented members of our family. I only found a few of the weaker ones. I started to demure because showing these notebooks would be embarrassing. But then I thought, "That is not what I am about. I am about the reality." At the conference, the persistent lady asked me again if I would show her the notebooks. As I pulled them out of my book bag, my heart was pounding with fear and dread. Now she would know what a fraud I was. As she leafed through them, she turned to me and said with tears in her eyes, "Thank you very much. For the first time I understand that I can do this in my family." This brought tears to my eyes.

That is what I want to say. That is what I want you to understand. You can do this. Don't make it harder than it has to be. Just because your drawings aren't lovely doesn't mean they aren't teaching you to see and pay attention. I have found in life that most of my efforts fall far short of the mark. But in the end, it is God that gives the increase. We take our baby steps in faith, trusting that those efforts matter, and God makes them matter.

Suggested Reading

Naming Nature by Mary Blocksma

Last Child in the Woods by Richard Louv

The Lost Art of Reading Nature's Signs by Tristan Gooley

The Laws Guide to Nature Journaling and Drawing by John Muir Laws (and others by the author)

The Living Page: Keeping Notebooks with Charlotte Mason by Laurie Bestvater

Nature Journaling by Clare Walker Leslie and Charles E. Roth

Home Economics by Wendell Berry (and others by the author)

Wintering by Katherine May

Books on the AT

Hiking Through: Finding Peace and Freedom on the Appalachian Trail by Paul V. Stutzman

A Walk in the Woods by Bill Bryson

Grandma Gatewood's Walk: The Inspiring Story of the Woman Who Saved the Appalachian Trail by Ben Montgomery

AWOL on the Appalachian Trail by David Miller

Becoming Odyssa: Adventures on the Appalachian Trail by Jennifer Pharr Davis

Balancing on the Blue: A Dromomaniac Hiking by Keith
  Foskett
Where's the Next Shelter by Gary Sizer

Growth Ideas

- Go outside. Right now.
- Buy yourself a nature notebook.
- Find a friend who knows more than you do about
  nature.
- Take a walk in the rain.

CHAPTER FIVE

The Active Mother

"It's a dangerous business, Frodo, going out of your
door," he used to say. "You step into the Road, and if
you don't keep your feet, there is no knowing where
you might be swept off to."

J. R. R. Tolkien, *The Fellowship of the Ring*

Healthy Habits

Close on the heels of the natural mother is the active mother. I
don't like to think of the active mother as the stereotypical gym
rat. In fact, I despise the modern idea that the ultimate discipline
comes at the gym. I like to think of the active mother as a woman
who pursues healthy habits in the midst of her ordinary life. Sure
we all go through extraordinary times where we might pursue a
big athletic goal like running a marathon (well, not me), but that is
not what this chapter is about. Balancing our own dreams of glory
and fitness with the everyday needs of our families is much more
complicated than going to the gym.

We moderns like to think we are entirely in charge of our own
destinies. This creates a tension in the life of a mother because
much of our life's course hinges on what happens with our family members. On any given morning, we might find ourselves on
the way to urgent care. This uncertainty is true for all people, but
mothers have the oversight of more than just themselves. This rais-

105

es the potential for more interruptions, and we all know that the potential and the reality are never far apart in a family.

This potential for interruptions is why establishing micro-habits is better than attempting dramatic change in the area of personal health. I am not a shining example of a fit, thin woman. I have relentlessly pursued information on these topics and have gained head knowledge but in the face of juggling my family's needs, I have often failed to be consistent. In my prime, I was not under as much pressure to be "hot" as women are now. As I have reached sixty, it is nice to be outside that rat race. Indeed, most women never get out of the starting gate in the race to be "hot" as apparently God has differing views of beauty than humans. Beauty is a wonderful thing, but ordering our values towards God's view of beauty will help us find contentment. This is hard to do because we have sensualized beauty, as if it only had one purpose.

> Beauty is a wonderful thing, but ordering our values towards God's view of beauty will help us find contentment.

> For the LORD sees not as man sees: man looks on the outward appearance, but the LORD looks on the heart. (1 Samuel 16:7b)

How many times have you met someone who was at first unattractive to you, but as you got to know them you were enchanted by their inner beauty so much that you forgot that they were not physically attractive? We will discuss beauty more in chapter eight.

And then we also have to ask ourselves how much time and money can we devote to our own physical appearance? This depends on how much time and money we have. For many large, one-income families, money is a constraint. Gym membership is out of the question, not just a matter of priorities.

Our grocery bill was always the biggest expense we had. I had to shop at discount stores and co-ops just to make it stretch. Going to a high-quality grocery store like Whole Foods or Publix was out of the question. Now I can afford to shop at those lovely stores, and because my old grocery bill was so high in the past, I don't notice that I am spending more. My son loves for his family to eat high-quality food, and his wife is a wonderful cook. Their grocery bill is their biggest expense on purpose.

No matter how much we believe all the adages about investing in ourselves, we don't always have the resources of time or money available to do what we wish. If so, finding little ways to enhance our physical appearance and health is more realistic. Anything we do that can be incorporated into real life is going to be more lasting. One good thing that has come out of the paleo movement is the idea of doing real things for exercise and eating real foods. When we think organically about life and relationships, we are in a better place to build lasting change. Ultimately, if we don't love what we are doing, we won't keep it up. But this doesn't mean we might not come to love some things we thought we would never love, like certain foods or forms of exercise.

Changing a habit is such a little thing, and yet all the force of the world stands against it. I think this is because stability is a good thing. It is good to build our house on the rock and not the sand, but sometimes we have to brave the winds and the sea to change our habits, especially if our house is resting in a dangerous place.

The safest way to keep our lives stable while effecting change is to only change one thing at a time. If you are a stay-at-home mom or a homeschool mom, you have already stood against the forces of culture. You have what it takes to change a bad habit or two. To change a habit is such a feat of character that the person who accomplishes it is empowered to make even more changes. I love the feeling of empowerment, "I can do anything," that comes when I successfully overcome a lifetime bad habit to remake myself into somebody new. Building a new habit is building a new person. That is kind of fun.

Exercise

A few years ago, in my forties and early fifties, I surprised myself by running a few 5K races. This was not a little thing for me. I hated formal exercise. I loved playing outdoor games and walking, but I hated the idea of getting up in the morning and exercising. My mornings were already my sacred contemplation and reading times. I didn't have time to squeeze in exercise, and when I tried I got anxious and irritable. But by my late forties, my last baby was reading on his own and some of my after-Morning-Time hours were freed up. I decided one day to try a "Couch to 5K" program, even though I didn't believe I could run or that I even wanted to run. To this day, I do not know why I did it. The first day I went out by the side road of our house and walked, adding in a tiny stretch of running, less than a minute. I could barely do it. I huffed and puffed and even cramped up immediately. I stopped right in the road and started crying even though I was out there with one of my sons who patted my back comfortingly. I limped home discouraged. Two days later, I did it again with the same result. This was insanity, and yet I just kept doing it. Maybe I just wondered if I was the same species of animal as my sons, who all seemed to be able to take on any sort of hard physical training. Eventually, one day, I ran very, very slowly—one mile. Within two weeks of that, I ran two miles. After that I signed up for a 5K and began several years of running, finally running 5 or 6 miles at a time.

The problem was I always felt like I had to run more and more and more until my body broke down, or the time running became unwieldy. I love the "Couch to 5K" program and found that whenever I quit running and came back to it, the run/walk scenario was the most fun for me. But now I realize that for balance and stability, it is better for me to just run/walk on a regular basis. This is something I can do in a short amount of time. I don't have to search the web for crazy running programs and crazy eating programs. I can just run a little bit in moderation a few days a week while I am walking. I can do that for the rest of my life, possibly, although life does have a way of interrupting the best-laid plans. This modest goal is fun and doable. It helps me stay in shape so that I can participate in things I love, like playing with my grandchildren or hiking some of the Tennessee hills.

All or nothing gets nothing.

In addition to the run/walk idea, I have found short exercise programs work better than elaborate ones. I have done a T-Tapp fifteen-minute workout several days a week.[1] I used to try to do this every single day, but then I completely gave up doing it. All or nothing gets nothing. I try now to incorporate strategies that keep me from giving up. If I faithfully do something when I can, I do not have to stress over the times when I can't. This is not because I lack grit, drive, or discipline. It is because I am a member of a family and a community, and my personal relationships often trump my own plans. Self-care should prepare us for service to others, not prevent us from helping them.

Walking

I am a sedentary person. I love being outdoors, but most of my hobbies require me to sit in a comfy chair with a cold or hot drink. I like to read and do puzzles and think and write. Audiobooks have helped me a little since I can walk and read at the same time, but overall I have to be purposeful to get the most basic of movement in my life.

> Self-care should prepare us for service to others, not prevent us from helping them.

Now that I have determined not to go crazy running, I have a Fitbit for walking. Ideally, I think it would be better not to have a Fitbit. It is a crutch which goes against my own better judgment, but for now it is a crutch I need. I used to get in about 8,000 steps a day, so of course, I changed my goal to 10,000 steps and then moved on to 12,000 steps. Once again I was following a pattern of failure. By ever increasing my goal I was headed for a crash and of course, in a moment of anxiety, I stuffed the Fitbit in a drawer.

Now my goal is much more modest, and it does not include frustration at myself for failing. Sitting by my dad's bedside at hospice was more important than getting in 10,000 steps (although I should have ditched the bag of peanut M&Ms).

Walking is the perfect exercise for the long haul. Most of us will be able to walk for our entire lives. If we love nature study, walking is the natural way to participate in that. I love going to our local park, Greenway, in the fall and walking the trails. A feeling of well-being washes over me as I walk. Walking doesn't require special equipment. I can walk in my flip-flops most of the time. I can even walk in the living and dining room of my small house. Four laps makes one hundred steps. I also own a high-quality treadmill which I found on Craigslist. Some people hate treadmills, but I love mine. I never have to join Planet Fitness again where I might be unlucky enough on a Sunday afternoon to be directly in front of *Naked and Afraid* or "plastic surgery mishaps" on the TV. Those images are indelible. I can listen to my audiobook or even watch something on Netflix from my basement treadmill. I don't feel nearly as guilty binge watching if I am on the treadmill.

The community of friends on my Fitbit is less distressing to me than having some old guy named Sergio offer me suggestions for exercise at the gym. I love being a part of daily and weekly group challenges, even though I mostly lose to Kristi, who is an insane walker, or Abby, who breaks all records during sheep shearing. I did win once by staying up until midnight walking for hours to win the challenge. I quit for a while shortly after that, though.

Walking is great for my mental health too. It gives me time to think and pray. I can write a chapter of a book in my head while walking, or I can pray for my children. I can watch the changing seasons and plan tomorrow's school day. I can get my dog, Max, to the park even though he is hard to walk with other dogs nearby.

He loves them all so much. I went on a Max sabbatical after he pulled me into a mud slick while trying to reach another dog. I slipped and fell, and Max got to greet his new bestie.

Walking is the perfect antidote to my sedentary lifestyle. In fact, it is 11:50 a.m., and I only have 1,500 steps for today. I'd better take a break from writing.

Play

My mother used to play with us. By "us," I mean our whole neighborhood. It sounds a little creepy now, but she used to pretend to be a witch and chase all the kids around our yard, tying us to the clothesline when she caught us. She swears now she only tied us loosely. In spite of the utter terror of this, kids flocked to our house. After developing this weird relationship, she often fed them all hot dogs and Kool-Aid. Eventually she started backyard Bible clubs, ending each club with one of her chases! My mother knew how to play. Today she would probably be arrested. Recently, a girl from our old neighborhood contacted me on Facebook to ask about my mother. This woman had not seen my mother in over 50 years, and yet she wanted to let Mom know how much she had changed her life for good. Who knew?

I wasn't quite as much fun as my mother when my kids were little. I did get on the floor and pretend to be a snake once, but I regretted it when the boys begged me for years afterward to do it again. The very nature of the word "play" implies fun. If it is fun, then it is play. Yet, we know that early childhood specialists consider play the work of children. I wonder if it is not the work of adults too. Persons.

I was a very shy child. I don't like to use the word "very" much, but I was extremely shy. My dad was a well-known coach in our community, and whenever I showed up for gym class I could see Coach Thomas's utter disappointment in me. I was too shy to play hard or well. Later in life, I gradually came out of my shell enough to try a few sports and found to my amazement that playing things like volleyball, kickball, and Wiffle ball was not terrifying but fun. In what felt like the safe environment of my own family, I learned to play sports with my children. I went sledding, even climbing Pierson's Hill in a dress to join the fun. What I learned from a lifetime of fear and self-consciousness is that play is so much fun because it gives us a chance to forget about ourselves. It is utter freedom from self.

> Play is utter freedom from self.

When I was a child of eight or nine years of age, and long before I knew I was an anglophile, I played croquet. Croquet has always been a happy place for me. I played it in a safe place, my grandparents' house. The deep love my grandfather had for me *and* for croquet gave me courage and joy. I could beat anyone at croquet, except my grandfather. When I wonder what play looks like, I think of croquet.

Recently, I have taken up golf. Not really. I have taken up *watching* golf. It is an outdoor sport, and those are the only sports I like. As I watch the players walk around the course, I wonder if I could play, even now after all these years. Could I play golf? I don't know. I am not very good at Putt-Putt golf, but seeing Facebook videos of old ladies doing amazing physical feats tempts me to try. At the least, watching golf is a great Sunday afternoon Zen experience.

What about you? How do you play? What activity frees you from self-consciousness, shows off your abilities, and brings you joy? Don't forget to play. Play is exercise too, and maybe the best kind of all.

Sunshine, Fresh Air, and Sports

As I mentioned above, I love outdoor sports. I love being outside in the sunshine and in nature too. I have seen some amazing sights while watching baseball games. Once a hawk was flying low over the field with a squirrel. He could barely keep himself in the air, and the game had to stop until he made it to the fence where he could rest before carrying the squirrel to his meal table.

> Play is exercise too, and maybe the best kind of all.

Watching our children play sports can be a rat race, but it can also be a sanity saver. I love sitting in the sunshine at a baseball game even though in the early spring the air is still quite cold. Baseball is a harbinger of spring. Sometimes my husband says, "You can stay home and rest today; I will represent our family at the game." I have never taken him up on this offer. What could be more restful than sitting at a baseball game taking all my frustrations out on an umpire?

Sports provide a way for us to get out of doors. They pull us away from our computers and devices (although I did write quite a bit of my book *Mere Motherhood* with a laptop at a baseball game), and they allow us to soak up some of that important vitamin D. Our indoor modern lives have left us depleted of this important vitamin. Even sunglasses can block the absorption of vitamin D since most of it is absorbed through the eyes and the skin. I love a cool pair of Ray-Bans, but they are better as a fashion accessory than something to wear while at a ball game. Even sunscreen can block cancer-killing vitamin D. Sunburns are never good, but a little sun is healthy, especially if it is gotten while doing something besides lying in a lawn chair with Hawaiian Tropic slathered all over you. Use the Hawaiian Tropic after a shower, if you need that beach-smell fix, and who doesn't need that?

We don't just need the sunshine of the outdoors, we also need the fresh air. Oxygen may contribute more to health than most of us realize. Of course, we know that we are dependent on oxygen every second of every day, but sometimes we are indoors more than we realize, and the health benefits of re-oxygenating our blood can be invigorating. Even sitting at a ball game can have health benefits if it is outdoors. Aerobic exercise may be healthful for this very reason; it helps our bodies oxygenate better. It's not just about burning calories. I have a friend who tapes his mouth shut at night in order to facilitate healthier breathing habits which promote better oxygenation of the blood, or so he says. I am not about to tape my mouth shut at night.

Charlotte Mason promoted the idea that we should be outdoors more than indoors. To get anywhere near this ideal, we have to be purposeful. Outdoor sports can help achieve this goal.

Outdoor sports are a great parenting tool. Our children are happier and healthier when they get lots of exercise and sunshine. Every little thing we can do to smooth out those hormonal puberty years for our children is important. More sunshine, fresh air, and exercise means less grumpiness. The first tool in the fight against depression is sunlight, for ourselves and our children.

If you tend to be a homebody who doesn't get out much, like me, having your children play an outdoor sport can bring surprising mental, physical, and spiritual benefits into your life.

I even know a few moms who took up an outdoor sport themselves. Moms can play softball, tennis, or the ubiquitous pickleball. Many cities have adult rec league sports now. My own adult daughter, Emily, recently signed up for a softball league, and I had the extreme joy of watching her play for the first time.

Do you have too many kids to have them all in a sport? Maybe they could watch you play a sport instead. My own childhood was spent at the baseball park where my father coached. It was a happy place, and I still follow that particular ball park, since remodeled, on Instagram.

Sleep

Was there ever a more elusive thing for a mother than sleep? My husband and I joke that after our first baby was born we didn't get a good night's sleep for twenty years. Sleep is all the rage these days. Our circadian rhythms apparently affect every area of our lives. I am more neurotic about checking the sleep statistics on my Fitbit than my step count. I used to just count the hours from when I went to bed to when I woke up and that gave me decent results. I could easily go to bed early enough to get eight hours sleep. But now my Fitbit tells me that a good portion of that time does not qualify as quality sleep. In order to get eight hours of quality sleep, I would need to go to bed even earlier than my 9:30 p.m. bedtime. What's more, if my Fitbit tells me I didn't get a good night's sleep, I suddenly feel more tired. I cannot imagine how frustrated I would have felt with this statistic when I had small children. There were days when three straight hours of sleep felt like a gift, and it was. All this focus on circadian rhythms should alert us to the dangers of modern life and help us make adjustments. Maybe we *do* spend too much time on the computer after the children go to bed. Maybe we *do* make poor choices regarding bedtime for ourselves. It is so tempting to enjoy the peace and quiet that descends when the children go to bed, even if we are a little less patient mama the next day. Too many choices like that, and we have built a life of grumpiness.

> Too many choices like that, and we have built a life of grumpiness.

But while this new awareness has many benefits, there are pitfalls with having too much information. If circadian rhythms are so important, maybe having children is a bad idea after all. It is simply very difficult to get a good night's sleep with children in the house. Just last night I was awakened at 1:30 a.m. with a fear that Alex didn't get home safely from pizza night with his friends. He hadn't texted me the usual "I'm home." I couldn't see his car in the driveway as I peered out the window. I wandered all over the house, except upstairs, looking for clues to his whereabouts when my husband mentioned his car was in the driveway. I looked at my phone again and saw that the text had gotten buried under a bunch of bank notices. Alex had been home since 10:30. He is not a baby or a toddler, but I was kept awake by my worries for him. What mother doesn't wake in the night to a series of worries for her children running through her mind? For a while, I used the method of counting backwards from five hundred when I was awakened at night unable to sleep; sometimes I breathe in through my nose, hold my breath for several seconds and breathe out through my mouth. Surprisingly, this often puts me to sleep. My newest go-to is turning on my Dwell app and falling asleep as I listen to the Bible.

The biggest joke in life has got to be that once all your children grow up and you are free to sleep, you can't. Perhaps those of us past menopause are called to keep the night watches in prayer. The Bible says that "He gives His beloved sleep."[2] I think that means that we may trust God for the right amount of sleep, trying to make good decisions about bedtime along the way. Once again we do our part, but God is the one who gives the increase. In this case, He gives the increase of sleep, one of God's nicest gifts. We can live our lives as mothers in frustration over not getting enough rest, or we can seek the giver of gifts and ask Him to supply this need.

A Woman I Know: Judy Ward

I had a hard time thinking of an active woman who is inspiring without being off-balance. I did not just want to tell you all about some super-fit mom who makes her physique the most important part of her life. That mom thinks working out and eating right can be chalked up to a disciplined life while another mom thinks being disciplined means reading the *Iliad* after the children are asleep instead of vegging on Facebook. It is hard to be balanced in this life, and we all like to pat ourselves on the back for whatever we manage to accomplish, whether it be avoiding sugar or conjugating Latin verbs.

While I was pondering whom to feature, I happened to visit my parents. While there, my mom asked me if I would like to take a walk with her. My mom, Judy Ward, is a dancer. A few years ago, she was teaching the Charleston to the young and old people who lived and worked at her assisted living home. In fact, when we met one April for my dad's birthday, she lined up all the great-grand-children and taught them to Charleston too. Put on dance music and she will dance. Several times during my childhood she opened up dance studios. I recently found an ad from a newspaper dated 1962 with her advertisement for teaching dance. My mom still has her tap shoes with the lovely satin ribbons, and it wasn't too long ago that she was tapping away.

Then she had the brain aneurysm. She was in the hospital for over a month and then rehab. She lost her short-term memory, her balance, and her love of chocolate, but she didn't lose her desire to dance. So today you will find her holding on to something and dancing whenever she hears the music. And to keep herself healthy, she walks every single day—rain, snow, or shine, although not ice. She loves to walk, and when she gets to an object she can hold onto, she pretends it is a ballet bar and stretches. Being a daughter, I have not always found all this walking charming. Sometimes it has been annoying. Sometimes, I felt she was prodding me to walk a little too much. Her walking made me defensive and grumpy. Being a daughter, that made me want to sit on the couch and eat chocolate until she came back from her walk. That is how life is for young women and older ones. But I am not so young anymore. My insecurities have been burned away with my own advancing years. When my mom says, "Would you like to take a walk?" I say, "Sure." Or maybe it is just that I am wearing a Fitbit, and I get some sort of credit for those steps!

What I love most about my active mother is that she doesn't walk or dance because it is good for her, she does those things because she loves them. That is the easiest kind of exercise program around.

The Ideal and the Reality

You don't have to look far in this culture to find ridiculous ideals of fitness and activity. Almost every picture of a woman in the media shows a perfectly fit lady in tight spandex or pretty yoga clothes. If you accept that as the ideal, then you are going to have to give everything you have to reach that goal, and when you have it, you are going to have to give everything you have to keep it. It is a relent-less message which keeps us focused on ourselves and our bodies at the expense of our minds and our spirits. Bodies are good and keeping them as healthy as we can is good, but keeping them so fine-tuned that we have time for nothing else is wrong. When we glance at the Benedictine life, we notice something else going on. We see a life based on balance and stability. Sure, we should care for our bodies, but undue stress on the body starves the mind and the soul. We must remember that we are not just physical creatures. We have a duty to care for what Hamlet called "this mortal coil," to enhance it, to cherish it, but we must beware of that old enemy whose favorite trick is sleight of hand. One minute you are caring for your body, and the next you are worshiping it in front of the mirror at the gym. Healthy habits come down to one word: moderation. When we enjoy something in moderation, we know that it cannot harm us.

Recently on our church prayer list, a woman asked for prayer as she began a weight loss program. There were lots of encourag-

> Healthy habits come down to one word: moderation.

ing comments and "atta girl" and "you've got this," but my favorite comment said it all: "Absolutely! You are so wise to ask for prayer support. Our Heavenly Father loves us just the size we are, but you are right—health matters. He absolutely wants us to take care of our bodies. He's got this!"

The reality for mothers is that balance is difficult. Motherhood is not for the weak. You will be tempted on every hand to forgo balance and pursue extremes, even extreme love for your children, yourself, and your husband. To be able to tune out this temptation to excess, which meets us at every turn of modern life, kind of makes us superheroes. Mary, you have chosen the better thing, and it will not be taken away from you.[3]

Suggested Reading

> *The Power of Habit* by Charles Duhigg
> *Better than Before* by Gretchen Rubin
> *The Wellness Revelation* by Alisa Keeton

Growth Ideas

- Buy a Fitbit and use it as a sleep monitor.
- Drink a lot of water.
- Cut out the carbs.
- Take a walk in the rain or snow.
- Find someone thinner than me and ask them.

CHAPTER SIX

The Studious Mother

Unexpectedly, it was Oxford that taught me it was
okay to be both feminine and smart, that intelligence
was, as a friend put it, a "woman's best cosmetic."

Carolyn Weber in *Surprised by Oxford*

Self-Education

Most homeschooling moms I know are studious self-learners. That
is not to say that all homeschool moms like to study, because I have
met a few who either sell themselves short as learners or would
rather just cook. Recently, in thinking about the AmblesideOnline Year 1 book list,[1] a list of books I have read aloud several times,
it occurred to me that no matter how smart I think I am, I always
learn something new while reading those first grade books. I say
"new," even though I have read them repeatedly now. Each time
I read a book, I take something new away. That is the beauty of
education. We are always adding to what we don't know. Here a
little, there a little. I cannot imagine a college-educated person not
getting something out of AmblesideOnline Year 1. Coming up
against the place where we "don't know" should make us excited.
This is where the learning begins. The student who breaks down
at this point is not a learner at all. No need to sell yourself short,
mom. We all start at the same place: "I don't know."

Over the years, I have run up against this place many, many times. From my first reading aloud about George Washington, to my everyday teaching of students, to my ordinary reading life, I am not just teaching; I am learning still. Sometimes, my reading leads me to think and ponder and consider, taking me to new places of thought, which then causes me to rethink things I have read before. I love that kind of learning. It makes my whole life feel fresh.

Other times, though, my learning is more purposeful. I have come up against the "I don't know" of a subject that captures my curiosity and sends me down the path of learning a new body of knowledge. This is empowering in quite a different way, because often tackling a new body of knowledge is quite difficult. Overcoming those difficulties, some of them having to do with age, makes me feel invincible. After tackling that first year of Wheelock's *Latin*, I almost felt like I could go to law school. Anything was possible with a little effort and study—or a lot. Since we don't have the time to tackle every subject like this, it is nice to be able to find other teachers for our children. But it is also nice, every once in awhile (and especially if we are short of money) to teach ourselves first what we want to teach our children. You can study a course from Khan Academy just as well as your children.[2] Not only does this empower you, but it also empowers your children. If you can do it, so can they. I also think it helps your older children to feel more respect for you. It illustrates that you are a person in your own right and

> I have come up against the "I don't know" of a subject that captures my curiosity and sends me down the path of learning a new body of knowledge.

therefore someone to be respected. Sometimes pubescent children forget that. Mom can become a bit cliché with her admonitions and household duties. A little pre-calculus can put her in a whole new light.

In the rest of the chapter, I am going to take you to the wood between the worlds where each subject of knowledge is a different pool. Remember that place in *The Magician's Nephew,* where mean Uncle Andrew sends Polly and Digory, and they discover that each pool leads to a different world? That is what learning is like. There are untold pools in this wood, and we can plunge in anywhere we like. We can explore one world fully and completely for the rest of our lives, or we can dip our feet in here and there. This chapter won't cover all those pools. How could it? These are just the worlds I have discovered so far.

Loving and Learning Shakespeare

My love of Shakespeare came naturally to me and quite by accident. My wide, eclectic reading during high school awakened me to the fact that Shakespeare was important. I felt a little cheated that the only play I knew anything about was *Romeo and Juliet* from my eighth-grade literature course. In an early hint of my future life, I bought a huge complete volume of William Shakespeare's works the year I was sixteen. I hardly know how this happened, except I have vague recollections of whining to my grandmother to buy it for me. But there it was in my room, and one day I picked it up and read *The Taming of the Shrew*. About halfway through, I realized it was written in some sort of meter. This utterly delighted me. It was such an epiphany that, to this day, I am sad when I have to steal that moment from students. Perhaps that is why I love Shakespeare while so many others have grown to hate the Bard. These early seeds would take many years to fully come to fruition in my life. Today, I like to continually have some work of Shakespeare going. I use a Shakespeare-in-a-year guide, but I rarely make it through the guide in one year. I just keep plugging away. In August of year two, I read *Measure for Measure*. My own reading of Shakespeare is quite apart from any readings I do with my students. In this way, I have read through some of the plays seven or eight times over the course of my life. My original plan consists of reading through all the plays in written form in the order they were written, followed by listening to all the plays by Arkangel audio recordings. Listening is somewhat more problematic than either reading or watching since you don't always know who is talking if the voices aren't distinct. I suggest having the written version at hand if you are not familiar with a play. Having finished both—reading each play and listening to each one—I am now continuing the project by watching each play on video while reading through Isaac Asimov's summaries in his wonderfully opinionated book Asimov's *Guide to Shakespeare*. I am currently slated to watch (or I should say rewatch) "Henry IV, Part 1" in the magnificent BBC film series *The Hollow Crown*. This will then prepare me for the grand finale of my Shakespeare Project: seeing each play performed live, some maybe in Stratford-upon-Avon and at the Globe in London.

There are many resources available for learning about Shakespeare and his plays. I will list a few of my favorites at the end of this chapter, but one of the most interesting things that comes up when studying Shakespeare is the vast number of people who like to argue about whether there ever was a Shakespeare or whether Shakespeare wasn't Shakespeare after all. This comes down to a simple argument. Could a man with "small Latin and less Greek" have written plays with so many classical allusions? Even though these detractors know that he did not make up his stories but harvested them from other famous works, works widely available in the sixteenth century, they still think he needed to have what amounts to a college degree to have written these plays. Can you guess that this deeply offends me? I feel so sad when I hear people say this because I see that they have missed all the beauty of Shakespeare. They have missed that he was an imitator, an actor. He was a man who paid attention. He didn't need Greek and Latin to write his plays; he needed to see people and show them to us. What scholar in an ivory tower could do that? Was there ever a better example of the fruit of what Charlotte Mason called the habit of attention than William Shakespeare?

A funny thing happened to me as I was reading Shakespeare's plays. I fell in love. I don't have this grand plan which spans the course of my life because I think I "should." I do it because I love the plays of William Shakespeare. I love his words. I love the way he shows me people and makes me laugh and cry over them. Shakespeare never loses the people in the story. It is always about the people, and what better way to portray the human soul than through the human heartbeat of iambic pentameter?

Dear friends, you come too!

Dear friends, you come too!

Shakespeare in a Year

Week 1 *The Two Gentlemen of Verona*, Sonnets 1-2

Week 2 *The Comedy of Errors*, Sonnets 3-4

Week 3 *Titus Andronicus*, Sonnets 5-6

Week 4 "Venus and Adonis"

Week 5 *The Taming of the Shrew*, Sonnets 7-8

Week 6 *Love's Labor's Lost*, Sonnets 9-10

Week 7 *King John*, Sonnets 11-12

Week 8 *Romeo and Juliet*, Sonnets 13-14

Week 9 *A Midsummer Night's Dream*, Sonnets 15-16

Week 10 "A Lover's Complaint"

Week 11 Sonnets 17-30

Week 12 Catch-up week

Week 13 Catch-up week

Week 14 *Richard II*, Sonnets 31-32

Week 15 *Henry IV*, Part I, Sonnets 33-34

Week 16 *Henry IV*, Part II, Sonnets 35-36

Week 17 *The Merry Wives of Windsor*, Sonnets 37-38

Week 18 *Henry V*, Sonnets 39-40

Week 19 *Henry VI*, Part I, Sonnets 41-42

Week 20 *Henry VI*, Part II, Sonnets 43-44

Week 21 *Henry VI*, Part III, Sonnets 45-46

Week 22 *Richard III*, Sonnets 47-48

Week 23 *The Merchant of Venice*, Sonnets 49-50

Week 24 *Much Ado About Nothing*, Sonnets 51-52

Week 25 *Julius Caesar*, Sonnets 53-54

Week 26 *As You Like It*, Sonnets 55-56

Week 27 "The Rape of Lucrece"

Week 28 Sonnets 57-70

Week 29 *Hamlet*, Sonnets 71-72

Week 30 Sonnets 73-85

Week 31 "The Phoenix and the Turtle"

Week 32 *Twelfth Night*, Sonnets 86-87

Week 33 *Troilus and Cressida*, Sonnets 88-89

Week 34 *All's Well that Ends Well*, Sonnets 90-91

Week 35 *Measure for Measure*, Sonnets 92-93

Week 36 *Othello*, Sonnets 94-95

Week 37-38 *King Lear*, Sonnets 96-97

Week 39 *Macbeth*, Sonnets 98-99

Week 40 *Antony and Cleopatra*, Sonnet 100

Week 41 *Coriolanus*, Sonnet 101

Week 42 *Timon of Athens*, Sonnets 102-103

Week 43 *Pericles*, Sonnets 104-105

Week 44 *Cymbeline*, Sonnets 106-107

Week 45 *The Winter's Tale*, Sonnets 108-109

Week 46 "A Funeral Elegy"

Week 47 *Henry VIII*, Sonnets 110-111

Week 48 *The Two Noble Kinsmen*, Sonnets 112-113

Week 49 Sonnets 114-130

Week 50 Sonnets 131-145

Week 51 Sonnets 146-154

Week 52 *The Tempest*

Grammar

My love of grammar was a long time coming—sort of. I didn't recognize that the love of words was the love of grammar. I loved words because they had form and meaning, and most especially nuances. I was in my forties before I realized that grammar also had a compelling form. It was a natural progression. After teaching several of my children phonics, I became enthralled with the order of it all. Sure, sure, English has so many exceptions, but moderns often call things exceptions because they just don't understand the rule. A child, or a mom, who learns phonics is well on her way to understanding logic. One other subject, at least, is tied up in the grammar of language, and that is history. An exception to a grammar or spelling rule is often just a story waiting to be heard.

I ended up learning far more phonics than my children learned because I kept seeking out more and more rules. This led me to spelling rules, and this led me to grammar. After all these years, I am still not a grammarian, but it is the depth of the subject which keeps me coming back—even the stories. Why do we have that archaic rule about never ending a sentence with a preposition? What about splitting infinitives? These rules all have stories to tell. While we should feel free to discard the rule when it becomes obsolete, it is important to know the stories. Those stories tell us the history of language.

In "The Natural Mother" chapter, we talked about the importance of knowing our natural world and its names: trees, flowers, shrubs, plants, shells, animals, birds. Naming nature is the beginning of knowledge. I learned the importance of this from two men who were not naturalists, but linguists. C. S. Lewis and J. R. R. Tolkien both recognized the importance of names. Names are parts of language, and when a name changes, it does so in a language. To know the grammar of a language is to understand the history of that language and even the stories of that language. Tolkien was a philologist, a lover of the *logos*. Lewis was more of an amateur philologist, which in itself means his love of *logos* (philology) was done out of love, not as a career or for money (he was an amateur). But these men, who both loved to name things and invented worlds in which they could continue naming things, came to the naming of things through the love of words—the grammar of language and its history. This makes the dry-as-dust subject of grammar come full circle to the nuances of poetry. Oh, frabjous day![3]

Once again, we are going to start this wonderful trek into the maze of language at the place where we don't know, but we can only do that when we admit that we don't know. Remember that archaic rule about never ending a sentence with a preposition? That rule doesn't make the least sense to a person who doesn't know what a preposition is. That person would be me, until well into my forties. Today I am likely to get so caught up in prepositions or infinitives that I run out of time to learn about other parts of grammar, but for most of my life the word infinitive was Greek to me.

So what is the story of prepositions? Is it really historically interesting? Grab a cup of coffee and settle in. A long time ago in a country racked by civil war and discontent, there lived a man named John Dryden (1631-1700). He was a serious man. The most celebrated author of his day, he became England's first poet laureate, a job he took as he took all things—seriously. You might have read his translation of Plutarch's *Lives*. Dryden, of course, was a Latin scholar and a complete grammar snob. He gazed at English with romantic eyes. This is not to say he blushed and batted, but rather, he preferred Latin (Roman) to English and over-applied his classical learning to the more vulgar (doesn't mean what you think it does) English.[4] Dryden noticed that English writers often ended sentences with prepositions. This is difficult to do in Latin because in Latin word order the preposition comes before the noun. Dryden found this form in his own writing as well as in others', and he felt it was "inelegant." He didn't set out to force his opinion on the English language, but he did mention his frustration here and there in passing. It just so happens that Dryden lived in a period of time when the English language was finally becoming formalized. And so, this little bit of classicism made its way into the new English grammar rulebooks, in spite of being a most unwieldy form. It has even been reported (most probably falsely) that Winston Churchill, that brilliant master of wit, said, "Ending a sentence with a preposition is something up with which I will not put." But that is another story.

I learn grammar now as I walk along the way. I pay attention when I hear a rule or when an author talks about grammar. I even, for the love of it, read grammar books. Not all of it sticks. But here a little, there a little, I am plunging into the adventure of grammar, and it is not dry at all. It is another pool in the wood between the worlds.

Latin

If you have a love of the English language and its grammar, phonics, and spelling, it will not be long before you run up against Latin. My own father told me over and over again how Latin was the most helpful thing he learned from his three years at Walnut Hills High School in Cincinnati, a classical public school. Dad encouraged me to take Latin in high school, but I never ended up doing that. I was such a late bloomer.

Almost with the very birth of the homeschooling movement came the idea of teaching children Latin. This posed a real problem: few people knew it. Many of us bought Latin programs and tried to muddle through them with our children, but it was tough going. At most we learned a smattering of Latin, a great many answers to crossword clues, and a whole bunch of chants. But with each new Latin program's appearance, improvements were made, and eventually Latin teachers who actually knew Latin began to surface. Along with those real Latin teachers, many co-ops began co-opting moms to teach Latin even though they still hadn't learned it themselves. Some of these co-ops charged a lot of money for classes taught by moms just learning Latin themselves. Relearning Latin was not going to happen in one generation. Thankfully, we are past that one generation now. Many of the moms I speak to now are second- and even third-generation home educators. Some of them did learn Latin. Some grew up to study it in college. Thanks to this, online Latin courses are now prolific.

> When we learn Latin, our grasp of English strengthens and, of course, our grasp of history.

The study of almost every subject is enhanced by the study of another subject. I have a theory that a cord of three subjects is the strongest education of all. When we learn Latin, our grasp of English strengthens and, of course, our grasp of history. Not only does the study of Latin introduce us to ancient Roman history, it helps us understand the Middle Ages, a time when monks preserved learning in monasteries, and even opens up to us the later generations, who built the Renaissance on classical models. While many consider Latin a dead language, it becomes hard to believe that idea when we run into it every single day in passing.

After years of throwing money at Latin programs and failing to make any headway, I decided one summer to take a course using Wheelock's *Latin* for myself. Being a busy mother of a large family, I didn't make it through the whole course, but I did gain enough Latin to help my children through their first year of Latin. Not only did it help me teach my children, but that semester of Wheelock's helped me learn to love Latin. I fell in love with the logic of the thing. I still hope to someday go back and complete Wheelock's *Latin* just for the fun of it.

The loveliest way to learn Latin is through singing it. Lovely Latin songs help us absorb Latin in a way that gives it meaning and beauty before we ever hit the books.

I have dabbled in the pool of Latin and found it to be a sparkling delight, paying back a hundredfold the investment. Even a little Latin goes a long way.

Writing

As a long time lover of words, it was inevitable that I should love to write. From my first meeting with Jo March eating apples in her garret with the rats, to my latest foray into the *Crosswalk Journals* of Madeleine L'Engle, I have been drawn to women who love to write. As a young girl I wrote poetry, and as a young wife I wrote stories imitating my friend, George MacDonald. (Yes, so many of my friends are dead.) My imitation, of course, was dreadful, but doing it taught

136

me a way of seeing life. As I became busy bearing and raising children, the only things I wrote were oral ditties that came to me as life steamed along—songs of babies and chores.

But then one day, a friend of mine wrote a blog post and sent it out. What was this? A place to write? And so I began a blog. The first day it had thirteen hits, most (or maybe all) my own. That began many years of blogging. I learned much about writing from blogging. I learned a bit of grammar when friends corrected me. I learned what people liked to read, which was mostly negative stuff, and I learned what I liked to write, which mostly nobody else liked to read. I learned to pay attention to criticism without letting my ego get in my way. I learned to make adjustments. When I read through those old blog posts today, I cringe. The thoughts are there, and the ideas, but the form is a mess. It was a process and a messy one. Even though I hate reading through those old posts now, knowing they desperately needed an editor, I love the lessons in writing I learned from blogging. Mostly they were lessons in thinking.

It turns out that blogging was close to what Charlotte Mason calls narrating. It was taking the things I was reading and thinking about and narrating it back to an audience. Blogging made me a better thinker and therefore a better writer. No writer starts out fully born. I am reading *Fear and Trembling* by Søren Kierkegaard right now, and I am struck by his youth. It reminds me of someone learning to write on a blog. He is living and learning and thinking and putting it all through the sieve of writing. He did not jump on the page as a full-grown existentialist. Writing is a process.

Writing is a process which will help most people learn to be better thinkers. It helps us formulate ideas and communicate them to others. Whether you keep a diary or a journal or a blog, doing so is not as much about developing your skill as a writer as it is about developing a way of learning to think. Writing is a shortcut to the depths of the mind. It helps us move from the shallow to the deep. The only problem is, once you learn to explore in those deep netherworlds of the mind, coming back to the shallows can be challenging. My husband is often slightly annoyed that I cannot make the transition more readily. I have learned to shake my head encouragingly rather than let him know his small talk did not compute.

As much as I love books about books, I also love books written by writers about writing. I will list a few of my favorites at the end of the chapter.

Philosophy

Philosophy is quite literally the love of wisdom. What self-respecting autodidact would not be interested in it? It is the bow that holds the entire package of education together. Even what we know of science and math contribute to this thing known as the Great Conversation. All of our knowledge, all of our naming of things, comes down to our ability to reach across time and space and make connections to ideas. Ideas are the food of the mind. They are everywhere. We can hardly help being philosophers, but the sheer proliferation of ideas makes our job all the harder.

Charlotte Mason via the Stoics reminds us that it is the job of the student to accept or reject initial ideas. Not all ideas are edifying. Some have wreaked havoc upon whole civilizations. Some say German philosopher Friedrick Nietzsche greatly influenced both the German people and Adolf Hitler. Nietzsche's *Übermensch* (super man) might only have been an initial idea hidden in a word to Hitler, but it was one that eventually took root in an evil mind and a collective consciousness. Some people think these ideas might have been the cause of World War II and the ability of the Germans to dehumanize Jews. Ideas have consequences.

The Bible speaks of understanding the times. We are called by theology to understand the ideas that drive (and sometimes plague) the culture of our own times. This does not mean we are called to change the culture. Individuals and ideas can change culture, but they do it almost always unawares. God's ways are mysterious. Daniel understood the Babylonian culture very well, and yet he did not start a petition to change it. He quietly went about worshiping the true God, and God turned that into something beyond any one man's doing. The key to culture change is in tiny, unconscious acts of faithfulness.

> Ideas are the food of the mind. They are everywhere. We can hardly help being philosophers.

To understand our own times, we have to look backwards to the stream of ideas that flow into Western culture. Some of those ideas are rich and good, some are tainted and poisonous. You can almost jump in anywhere and then move backwards and forwards through the stream of the ages. Sometimes it is easier to find a modern author to point you in the right direction.

Russell Kirk is a great place to start if you want to explore the ideals of American civilization specifically and Western culture generally. His book, *The Roots of American Order*, helps us understand that we did not come to this place called the United States of America by accident. He traces the roots of Western civilization through the great cities that made up that civilization—Athens, Rome, Jerusalem, and London. Politics is in many ways just the working out of ideas. Ideas have consequences, and consequences have ideas. Now that we live in a time of disordered thoughts, there has never been a better time to trace the roots of American order.

We could also trace the roots of educational thought through the centuries—from Socrates, Plato, and Aristotle; to Boethius, Comenius, and Charlotte Mason; and on to Stratford Caldecott and David Hicks. Each of these contributors to the Great Conversation causes us to ponder what it means to be human. *What is man? How do humans learn? Can beauty change the world? Can man be good? Evil?* So many questions that we are still pondering over thousands and thousands of years. It will humble you to wake up in the morning with your wide-eyed three-year-old gazing at you, trusting you to tell him all about the wonder-full world. Philosophy will remind you that "just the facts" is not going to cut it. That two hours he spent watching an ant yesterday is an act of philosophy on some level. Oh, the thoughts he will think!

One stream of philosophy flows into another. There are no islands. One idea leads to another, and one book leads to another. Philosophy is a journey that will take us places we know not. It is a part of every single thing we read, discuss, or watch, from a Terence Malik movie to the Braves and the Reds in extra innings, from Plato's *Republic* to *Gone with the Wind*. Philosophy, like nature, is always there; it is our eyes that need to be opened. How many trees do you fail to notice on your daily walk? How many nuances of thought do you miss while reading *Gaudy Night*? The habit of attention belongs to both the outward flora and fauna around us and the deep, hidden roots of thought that turn the world upside down. It is our attention that makes the difference. Often we are the blind being led by the blind, but when our eyes are opened, we begin to see men and trees.

Annie Dillard says:

> I think, that beauty and grace are performed whether or not we will or sense them. The least we can do is try to be there.[5]

Philosophy enhances our instincts and helps us to recognize those among us who are wolves in sheep's clothing. Perhaps it can help us become like Curdie in *The Princess and Curdie*, understanding just what kind of animal the shapes around us called humans are becoming. If you don't know what that alludes to, you will definitely want to read *The Princess and Curdie*. The Bible speaks about this in Mark 10:16, "Behold, I am sending you out as sheep in the midst of wolves, so be as wise as serpents and innocent as doves."

One of my favorite resources for understanding the times we live in is the *Mars Hill Audio Journal*.[6] It is a great place to listen to ideas, and those ideas will give you much to ponder. It is also a great place to find excellent books on philosophy and thought.

On some level, we are all philosophers; we love to think about something. Maybe it is just what our next meal will be. But if we take the time to wonder and ponder, our eyes will open our hearts to thoughts we never knew before. These will not be new thoughts but old ones. Old thoughts will become old friends, and we will begin to see the world and everything in it through fresh eyes. We will have friends who were born thousands of years before us and some yet to be born.

Science and Mathematics

I did not always love science nor mathematics. They seemed strangely precise. They offered no wiggle room like I found in ideas and literature, no room to ponder and wonder. As a consequence, I didn't do the best job of giving my children a love for these things or modeling it. I suppose, during those busy, busy years, I only had energy to pass on what I already loved. I think that is okay, but sometimes now I get glimpses of the beauty of the exact, and I am sad. Sad for myself as I watch the sand in the hourglass and sad for my children who were in some ways shortchanged. But to harken back to chapter one, I remember that we all start where we "don't know." How did I, a lover of logic puzzles, not find math sooner? What happened between all the fun I had as a teen in Algebra I and my complete math idiocy while raising my children? Perhaps it was geometry. I was well into my forties before I looked at trigonometry long enough to realize it was about triangles. That could only have happened if I had turned my attention off very early along the path to math. Sometime in tenth grade, I stuck my fingers in my ears and hummed a tune in double time while the teacher explained theorems. Perhaps it is not the job of the teacher to make every child love a subject—that would be impossible— but at the very least it should be her job to not make them hate it. Or maybe it was just fear. We cannot love what we fear. Why do so many people fear math, or science, or even poetry? What are we afraid of? Maybe it is the fear of failure. Maybe it is the fear of looking stupid. Maybe it is the fear of the incomprehensible.

When working a difficult logic problem, there comes a place where you have all the information, but it doesn't add up to a solution. Here is the test of our puzzle mettle. In my younger years, here was the place I got frustrated and angry with the puzzle makers. They had failed to give enough information! It was their fault, not mine. I turned to the answers at the back of the book. The answers always hinted to me that maybe I had all the information I needed. The puzzle wasn't lacking anything, I was. Now that I am older, I relish that place. That is the place where the magic happens. One minute I am at a dead end with no hope of figuring out a solution, and the next my brain is scrambling through all the information looking for patterns. The longer the search for answers, the more satisfying it is when they come. I learned that doing logic puzzles! It made me realize that I had given up on math and science prematurely. The consequence of my lack of grit in the maths and sciences was a deficit in wisdom and knowledge. But as with all learning, all is not lost. Time may be running out, but there is always Khan Academy.

A Woman I Know: Beth Harvey

Whenever I start talking about Beth Harvey, she thinks I am just being kind to her. She doesn't realize how much I love her story. Beth is the mother of three boys. She is a well-educated, articulate woman who is also an artist—at least she is now, and she was before she had children. To look at the lives of her three adult sons now, you would think that raising them must have been a breeze and that they must have all been geniuses who loved to learn right from the start. But Beth's boys happened to be real boys, and while they were wrestling and sometimes ignoring her, she just went right on learning herself.

Beth's boys happened to be real boys and while they were wrestling and sometimes ignoring her, she just went right on learning herself.

She decided to teach them Latin. While the boys did not fall in love with Latin, Beth did! Beth says, "If you lead a horse to water and he doesn't drink, drink it yourself." Beth became a true Latin scholar. She took online courses from Dale Grote and eventually started teaching Latin herself. She even ended up writing a Latin program. She has run an online tutorial for homeschoolers which especially caters to moms who want to learn too. And she is back to painting. Beth's example of being a lifelong learner did affect her boys. Not only are her boys each uniquely gifted and pursuing a life of learning, but even her husband has thrown himself into some of Beth's intellectual pursuits. The whole family has been enriched because Beth just kept on learning.

A Woman I Know: Kelly Cumbee

Over the years, I have gotten to meet in person many people I first encountered online. Sometimes these meetings have been disastrous, but sometimes they have been fruitful. Some of the girls who had read my blog for intellectual stimulation and book suggestions ended up far surpassing me in wisdom and knowledge. My cache of highly intelligent friends is ridiculously large, and I begrudgingly have to thank the internet for that. Kelly Cumbee is one of my oldest cyber-friends, and she has far surpassed me in the area of self-education. Kelly has several children, but she still finds time to pursue her own self-education through reading and taking online courses. She really does use the Open University![7] Kelly loves truth, beauty, and goodness, and you can tell by the way she orders her life. She takes ordering her affections seriously, and she has worked relentlessly for years acting on her convictions. As a consequence, she is one smart cookie.

The Ideal and the Reality

Years ago I had a blog post titled "The Composite Homeschooling Mom." It was about how we create in our minds the perfect home-schooling mother by cobbling together all the great things we see other moms doing. We measure ourselves against the best of each area. We want to teach math like that mom, or science like that one, all while doing beautiful handicrafts, keeping the house clean, and reading hundreds of books a year. The homeschool version of a Stepford wife. This creates much anxiety. It is like being in the wood between the worlds and frantically jumping in and out of each pool, never able to truly know or love any of the worlds we visit. That is sad. No individual mom will ever excel in every area. I am not a Latin scholar like Beth; I merely dabble. I do not have time to take Open University courses like Kelly, no matter how well I order my days. My days are different from Kelly's. We might be able to achieve "anything," like our culture constantly promises us, but we cannot achieve "everything." In this chapter, I shared a few of my own scholarly loves, but the list of possible intellectual pursuits is endless.

In his semi-autobiographical book, *The Power of One*, Bryce Courtenay writes of a 7-year old boy, PK, who spends his days on the cusp of World War II in South Africa with a German professor of music. They walk the hillsides collecting and recording plant specimens. They take pictures. They draw. They use the Latin names. The professor is adamant that the little boy record everything, and he is adamant that they sit and wonder. Later the little boy is called on to write an affidavit on behalf of the professor, and the judge does not believe a small boy can remember such details. But in fact, this small boy has been educated to be observant. To be attentive. To be precise. Later when he goes to school, they can hardly find a grade for him because he is so advanced. He has only studied music and botany with the professor, and yet he is far ahead of his peers in every subject. The deep knowledge that PK has learned in those two subjects transfers to every single thing he learns later.

The good news, as Charlotte Mason reminds us, is that education is the science of relations. When we spend time drinking deeply from one well, we often find that we have learned about many others, too. As countless homeschool moms grow up, and their thirst for wisdom and knowledge increases, vendors who originally only offered programs for children are now offering selections for moms and dads. This is a wonderful development. While we can't learn everything, we can learn something. Even at my age, I find this exciting.

See you at the library.

Suggested Reading

The Day I Became an Autodidact by Kendall Hailey

The *Phaedrus* by Plato

The Idea of the University by John Henry Newman

The Death of Christian Culture by John Senior

The Great Tradition by Richard M. Gamble

The Mind of the Middle Ages by Fredrich R. Artz

A Little Manual for Knowing by Esther Lightcap Meek

The Twilight of American Culture by Morris Berman

Beauty in the Word by Stratford Caldecott

Norms and Nobility by David Hicks

The *Home Education* series by Charlotte Mason,
   especially Vol. 6, *Towards a Philosophy of Education*

Suggested Resources on Shakespeare

Asimov's *Guide to Shakespeare* by Isaac Asimov

Shakespeare After All by Marjorie Garber

The Oxford Companion of Shakespeare edited by Michael
   Dobson and Stanley Wells

Shakespeare: The Essential Reference to His Play, His Poems, His Life and Times and More by Charles Boyce

The Arkangel Shakespeare Recordings, available on
   Audible

Upstart Crow (A BBC television show, which those
   already familiar with Shakespeare, will adore. Inappropriate for children.)

The Reduced Shakespeare Company—The Complete Works of William Shakespeare (Not for everyone, but hilarious if you already know the plays.)

Kings and Queens of England & Scotland by Plantagenet Somerset Fry (You are going to need this for the English history plays.)

My Ten Favorite Shakespeare Movies

1. *The Taming of the Shrew* (1967) with Richard Burton (no, John Cleese is not better) and Elizabeth Taylor.

2. *As You Like It* (2006) produced and directed by Kenneth Branagh.

3. *A Midsummer Night's Dream* (1935) directed by Max Reinhardt and William Dieterle, starring James Cagney, Mickey Rooney, Olivia de Havilland.

4. *Much Ado About Nothing* (1993) directed by Kenneth Branagh, starring Kenneth Branagh, Emma Thompson, Denzel Washington.

5. *Hamlet* (2009) directed by Gregory Doran, starring David Tennant, Patrick Stewart.

6. *Henry V* (1989) directed by Kenneth Branagh, starring Kenneth Branagh, Derek Jacobi, Simon Shepherd, and others. Neither Laurence Olivier's (1944) nor Tom Hiddleston's (*The Hollow Crown*, 2012) compare with Branagh's, although both are very good. Mark the music.

7. *Twelfth Night* (1996) directed by Trevor Nunn, starring Helena Bonham Carter, Richard E. Grant,

Nigel Hawthorne, Ben Kingsley.

8. *Hamlet* (1996) directed by Kenneth Branagh, starring Kenneth Branagh, Derek Jacobi, Julie Christie, Kate Winslet.

9. *The Life and Death of King John* (1984) from the BBC Television Shakespeare directed by David Giles starring Leonard Rossiter.

10. *The Hollow Crown* series, but especially "Richard II" (2012).

Books on Writing

The Writing Life by Annie Dillard

The Crosswalk Journals by Madeleine L'Engle

The Art of Memoir by Mary Kart

On Writing: A Memoir of the Craft by Stephen King

Dialogue with an Audience by John Ciardi

Bird by Bird by Anne Lamott

A Moveable Feast by Ernest Hemingway

Write Away: One Novelist's Approach to Fiction and the Writing Life by Elizabeth George

The Habit of Being by Flannery O'Connor

Talking About Detective Fiction by P. D. James

Poetics by Aristotle

The Getaway Car by Anne Patchett

Political Philosophy

The Roots of American Order by Russell Kirk

Liberal Fascism by Jonah Goldberg

Ideas Have Consequences by Richard Weaver
The Birth of the Modern by Paul Johnson
The City of God by St. Augustine
The Year of our Lord 1943 by Alan Jacobs

Growth Ideas

- Take a course though the Open University.
- Teach yourself math using Khan Academy.
- Use your Audible credits to buy a few Great Courses selections.

CHAPTER SEVEN

The Creative Mother

I like a cook who smiles out loud when he tastes his own work. Let God worry about your modesty; I want to see your enthusiasm.

Robert Farrar Capon

Homemaking as Art

Years ago on my blog I did a series on Edith Schaeffer's *The Hidden Art of Homemaking.* Edith's book is a lovely, if dated, look at the beauty we create in our homes. It inspired me to find dignity in the everyday tasks seemingly on autopilot in my home. Where the world saw drudgery, Edith saw a palette. I read *Hidden Art* on the heels of reading Dorothy Sayers's *The Mind of the Maker,* and truly they were kindred. Sayers's book revels in humans as sub-creators under God. We create because we were made by a Creator. Edith comes along and warns us not to forget the dignity of creating a home. How could we forget the dignity of that? How could the most central theme of human existence, the home, have lost its beauty and dignity?

Creativity is a longing in our hearts. This longing requires time and contemplation. Both mastery and creativity require time. Think of your home as a monastery preserving culture in a dark age. In spite of the fact that all the devils in hell conspire against the stay-at-home-mom and devalue her contribution to society, I am here to remind you that when all the dust settles and the books are opened there will be a reckoning. Your worth is far above jewels. Live for the final "well done," not the earthly valuation of your role as a mother or a homemaker. It is a sick society that misunderstands the value of the home. It is a sick society that values material goods over children. This reminds me of a quote by John Senior; he did not pull any punches.

> But the chilling truth is that industrialism brings on a paralyzing gluttony and greed in which the quality of life is quantified. Paradoxically, you cannot afford to have children in the affluent society. The world has never been so rich and wretched as in these air-conditioned Edens where another child would sap the payments on the second car. There is no population bomb today. Quite the opposite: the question is whether industrialized society can reproduce itself at all.[1]

Not only is having many children expensive and impractical in an affluent society, even having one child is highly counterproductive. The Bible has a verse that answers this charge, and it is one that I said over and over to myself while raising my children. Proverbs 14:4 says, "Where no oxen are, the crib is clean: but much increase is by the strength of the ox" (KJV).

There is an easy modern way to keep your house clean. Don't have children, and work all the time so that you are never at home. Then you can decorate in the popular cool toned colors like white or gray and have Pottery Barn white couches. There will be no fingerprints on the walls, no stains on the upholstery, and no crying in the background. Your sterile palette will be free from disease and failure and all the things true creativity feeds on. You will have plenty of time to binge watch other people's messes.

If you are reading this book, it is likely you have chosen the beautiful, creative mess. It is likely that your walls have lovely pictures carefully chosen and marker scribblings and dirt smudges. It is likely that the wood floor under your dining room table is sticky. It is likely that your couches are strong and old—and maybe even smell like one too many dirty diapers has been changed on them. It is likely that the view from your windows is lovely, although tainted with finger- and noseprints from a not-too-healthy child or two —or three. Perhaps you find yourself scrolling Pinterest and fantasizing over those pristine homes. Maybe your modern farmhouse look is a little too authentic.

Was that a mouse?

This brings us to the questions, "What is beauty? Is beauty in the eye of the beholder?" If the beholder is God, then the answer is yes. We see through a glass darkly. We cannot always know what is beautiful. Beauty is the old woman giving everything she had although it added up to almost nothing. The Bible tells us that God does not see as we see. His Pinterest boards would not look like ours. We often only see the back of the tapestry, and it looks like a big giant mess. One of the most challenging verses in the whole Bible is Psalm 50:21a: "You thought that I was altogether like you" (NKJV). Ouch. I did, I did.

So here we are, plopped right down into the chaos of a home with children, and what are we required to do? We are required to create! We are our Father's children after all. We were created, and we must create. Creating a home is one of life's simplest and most challenging projects. Without wisdom, we cannot do it. Without wisdom, we scream at our child for breaking our china. Without wisdom, we cannot fathom another sink of dirty dishes. Only wisdom understands that the laundry will be caught up one day. Only wisdom knows when to mop the floor and when to read a poem. And wisdom sees that sometimes we say the poem *while* we are mopping the floor.

> The glory is not in the perfect room; the glory is in the joy of providing a home for our imperfect family.

God has placed the atmosphere of our homes in our hands. As with all of life, this requires balance. We must see the dignity of cleaning our home and the dignity in making it dirty again. We must not despise the chores we must do, but we must find dignity in them. It is good to clean your home, to freshen your sheets, to set your table with pretty blue dishes, to open the windows, and watch the curtains flutter in the breeze. It is good wake up in the morning to a fresh palette on which to create the beauty of the day. There is honor in tackling that pile of laundry that Luanne Shackelford called Mount Neverrest.[2] Sure, it will be there again tomorrow, but it is easier to tackle it when we see that there too is beauty. Sometimes we are ahead on our chores, and often we are behind. It is a beautiful thing to keep on plowing ahead because we know it is easier to study and think in a somewhat clean environment rather than in a pig sty. The glory is not in the perfect room; the glory is in the joy of providing a home for our imperfect family. Some days this is more challenging than others. Some days, for all our work from sun up to sun down, there is no visible improvement. This is only because we cannot see the other side of the tapestry. Some day you will see it, and it will be beautiful.

The Lost Art of Mealtime

I have never met a set of dishes, nor a sandal, that I did not like. Perhaps it is an example of finding beauty in unexpected places, but I love dishes. They are unwieldy and hard to store, but it is hard for me not to revel in picking out pretty plates. It started with Blue Willow-patterned china. My grandmother owned these iconic dishes, and I inherited some of her pieces. Whether it was because I ate her delicious food off classic Blue Willow plates, or because food genuinely looks better on Blue Willow's beautiful blue and white scenic design, I do not know. But, if I go out of my way to make something special, like pancakes for breakfast, or cookies, or spaghetti pie, I must serve it on a blue plate. If you scroll through food pictures online, it almost seems to be a universal principle that food looks better on blue plates. Sometimes a nice red toile looks nice too, but never quite as stunning as blue. I was recently visiting my oldest son's house, and I was happy to see his wife was collecting Blue Willow too. It seems to be a tradition of beauty. Our meals may be simple and cheap, but they can always be pretty on a blue plate.

Cooking has always been problematic for me because I am not naturally thin. I come from a long line of chubby people. I used to counteract this problem by starving myself for days at a time, but when I had children, this wasn't very practical because it made me grumpy. Sometime after I turned thirty, I decided that it would be better for me to eat and be cheerful, but in recent years I have gone back to intermittent fasting, which is so much easier when there aren't children around to snap at. My husband might have to choose between a grumpy, skinny wife or a pleasant, chubby one. My guess is that in the long run, in spite of our workout culture, cheerfulness is more valuable to men than thinness. But I suspect there is a happy middle ground in some Edenic world which I have not found yet. Nevertheless, I maintain. I will not be two hundred pounds, and I will not be one hundred thirty either. I will not be snappy and grumpy all the time, but I will not be quite cheerful all the time either. My dear husband has to live with me, and I have to live with myself.

But back to cooking meals. Without a doubt, this is an area where much creativity can bring rich rewards. A couple of basic cookbooks and a couple of fancier ones, and that is really all any good cook, needs especially with the internet. Sometimes I can look up an old favorite recipe faster on the internet than by walking over to my cookbook shelf. Still, if there is a zombie apocalypse, I might need hard copies. The younger generations reading this book are probably doing a far better job of offering whole-food, delicious meals than I ever did. I know all of my daughters-in-law are excellent, healthy cooks. They don't rely on casseroles and biscuits like I did. I may know how to feed a crowd, but they know how to do it using whole foods. My favorite whole foods are butter, butter, and butter and cream.

After so many years of cooking for a crowd, I did lose inspiration. It is hard for me now to get up much gumption for cooking.

I am still a pretty good baker and have rested my reputation as a grandmother on the art of making cookies. However, the daily grind of meals has left me in a lull. Life's seasons change, and when I suddenly found a gallon of milk sour in the refrigerator, I woke up to the fact that I no longer knew what I was doing in the kitchen. You could say I have taken a sabbatical.

I still envision my husband and myself walking the aisles of Publix or Whole Foods, where shopping *is* a pleasure, in our cardigans and tennis shoes, picking out fresh food for our solitary meals. I imagine us savoring each bite after chopping and cooking the meal together, drinking a glass of wine, like some couple from a Netflix Original series who seem to have more than their fair share of hours in a day—but this has not materialized yet. I am also a bit distracted by all those new meal delivery services, which I have noticed use a lot of blue plates in their ads. Good call.

> . . . family meals are one of the easiest *and* hardest ways you can preserve the culture.

But if you are in the middle of those intense parenting years, take heart that even your chicken drumsticks can be served beautifully (if you have blue plates), and that family meals are one of the easiest *and* hardest ways you can preserve the culture. Easy because your family has to eat; hard because as your children age, the call away at dinner time hours is a siren very hard to resist. Mealtimes are indeed a lost art. If you manage to get a meal on the table, and if you manage to get all your family to sit down and eat it together, then you have managed to produce a work of art. You get to wake up and do it again tomorrow, and that is a beautiful thing.

Gardening

One of the most joyful applications of practicing beauty in the home comes from gardening. Gardening gets at the heart of everything that is true and good and beautiful, and it is practical because it is fruitful. Gardening can take us back to Eden (need I say peonies), and it can remind us of the fall (not every crop succeeds).

> Gardening gets at the heart of everything that is true and good and beautiful, and it is practical because it is fruitful.

Gardening gives us a chance to decorate our homes in gorgeous colors from simple things like zinnias, and it also gives us a chance to test our mettle against weeds. Weeds abound. It takes a certain amount of grit to weed a garden in the middle of August in the south. I have found that quite often if you have been diligent with the chore of weeding in May and June and some of July, you can just give up in August. Maybe God made it that way. The garden itself can be structured and beautiful, or bohemian and beautiful. It can even be a big fat mess, but what comes out of it into our homes is profound—whether it is the most prolific zucchini despised for being abundant, and yet the perfect toddler crop, or the more delicate spring asparagus, here today and gone tomorrow. When our tables are adorned with what we grew ourselves, all of life aligns in a cacophony of deep meaning. To have a table adorned with wildflowers purposefully grown for their ethereal beauty, pickles we have seasoned ourselves, and tomatoes whose flavor cannot be duplicated by the grocer is one of the rare treasures of life. To share with our families the joy of gardening is to pass along the beginnings of creation to them. To remind them that every single gardening metaphor from the beginning of time until now serves to help us understand how the world was made and by whom.

In my current season of life, I live in the shade, in a woody glen. For the past couple of years, I grew what I could of flowers and tomatoes on my back porch. It is always nice to have at least one thing growing nearby that I have planted with my own hands. But recently as spring approached, I was called away to attend to my dying father. It was not the year for growing things. It was the summer of dying. I do not say the summer of *death,* because death has no sting in Christ. My father defied his doctors in the spring and defied them again and again all summer long. He did not defy them forever. Because I was far from home many of those summer days, I bought a stone container filled with succulents, those plants that do not need to be watered regularly. I did not go so far as to buy fake succulents, even though they are almost identical to the real ones. To put a living thing in your home to grow may be absurd, but to put a fake one in is to verge on insanity. Fake things are reminders of real things. If you can have the real thing then you don't need a reminder.

This is true in the spiritual realm also. When we finally have Christ in our presence, when we see Him face to face, there will be no more need of even such a life giving force as our sun. There will not be a little bit of bread and wine in heaven; there will be a feast.

I am not the best gardener. I do not have a green thumb. I do not enjoy putting up food as much as I enjoy eating fresh food. But I do love flowers. This year I have twice paid over $40 to have fresh flowers cascading throughout my home. It was a ridiculous expense, but I do not regret it one bit. Both of my grandfathers eventually turned their entire large yards into gardens. Both of my grandmothers spent their summer days in the kitchen boiling mason jars filled with the harvest. When my maternal grandmother, Mammaw, opened a jar of blackberries in the winter, my heart could hardly contain the joy. When either of my grandfathers sat down for a meal, summer or winter, you could see the joy their hard work brought to the table. What modern web-surfer or binge-watcher ever feels that sort of reward? Gardening is closely related to the art of mealtime, both in the food that we prepare and the flowers we use to adorn our tables. Also, purple cabbage makes a very nice centerpiece with grapes cascading over the edge of the container.

When we owned a farm, we had a large garden which eventually I gave over to more and more flowers. We also had grapes. While I was not very good at putting up food, I somehow managed to make jelly. It must be super easy. It is super easy! You boil sugar and juice and pectin and *voila*, you have Christmas gifts, if you can keep your family from devouring it. I was never good at keeping my family from devouring anything. They were always so darn hungry. But in theory you can give away the work of your hands, and it will be more satisfying than an Amazon gift card. Last summer our neighbors, the Johnsons, who have the cutest kids and the cutest parents, gave us strawberry jam. With only three people at home, we still devoured that stuff in three days flat!

It will be a sad day when people no longer have gardens. If you don't have one, I highly recommend you try growing something this year. Two years ago, after Thanksgiving, I threw all the old pumpkins which I had used for decorating (and I had really gone overboard on pumpkins) into the ditch beside our house. Last summer I noticed a few vines creeping into the lawn from the ditch. Turns out I was growing pumpkins like Jack's beanstalk. I couldn't wait for my granddaughters to visit so that I could show them. Taking their cue from me, they get pretty excited about these sorts of things. This year they got even more excited when they saw the dead raccoon carcass in the woods, but I didn't grow that. Who would grow a rodent?

Gardening is the simplest and the hardest thing we can do to get in touch with true beauty in our homes. It is one of those essential things that help us understand what it means to be a human made in the image of the Creator. Now go out there and kick dirt.

The Art of Holy Days

I like to think of holidays as they were originally intended to be—Holy Days. As Christians who read through the Scripture, it doesn't take us long to notice how important Holy Days are in both the Old and the New Testaments. Jesus himself followed his nation's calendar of days, and no wonder since they all pointed to him. God's kindness is reflected to man in his provision for us to celebrate. I used to get mad at magazine writers who suggested we eat and eat and eat all during the Christmas holidays and then suggested that maybe we needed to go on a diet in January. Were they manipulating us? Maybe, or maybe they were just working within the natural order that God created. A time to feast and a time to fast.

In our family, we weren't good at all holidays. I have been told our birthdays were blasé, but we were very good at some holidays and conflicted with a few more. From Thanksgiving to Christmas, our home was one big festival of music, food, decorations, and meaning. I loved it, and my children did too. We could hardly wait for the season. It was never, ever about just the day. I love seeing that my children all grew up to carry on this love for the season of celebrating. It was this love that led me to share our traditions in the book *Hallelujah: Cultivating Advent Traditions with Handel's Messiah*, so I won't rehash how we celebrated those holidays here.

There are other days in both the church and on the secular calendars that lend themselves to refreshing our spirits and helping make our ordinary days more meaningful. Celebrating as a family is one of the most meaningful ways to solidify your family culture. Celebrating with your church family or your neighbors also solidifies the importance of community to your children. Sticking with our imperfect communities can help our children learn that life has permanence. I am sorry to say that we learned this the hard way, although I do admit there are still good reasons to leave a community, just not as many as we thought. And therein lies the heart of the holidays—it is hard to celebrate alone. Even the Lord's Table, our weekly Christian celebration, is communal. It is not meant as a private time of personal introspection, but rather a communal time of mutual recognition that each one of us needs both repentance and a Savior and that none of us rises above the others.

Celebrating the holidays in a family is an art. While it is joyous and fun, it can also be taxing and overwhelming to a mother. It can feel like it is "all up to me," and that attitude drives people away from us. I am sure most children and husbands would say they would rather have less merrymaking than a tired, grumpy mother.

But I have also found that when I say, "Okay, I will just buy the pies," everyone freaks out. So there is the art—creating a happy holiday without overdoing it and crashing.

One important thing we can remember is that seasons change. This has been especially difficult for me. Our Thanksgiving used to be our main day to be together as a family, and then my oldest son and his family moved to Japan. Then my other children's families had conflicts of scheduling, and suddenly our Thanksgivings were shrinking. Rationally, I understood that this was a normal shift in life, but suddenly, instead of Thanksgiving being a lovely holiday, it felt like something I had to panic over. And quite frankly, it hurt; I loved our old Thanksgivings. I miss them. Learning to deal with the changing nature of holidays and traditions is part of aging gracefully. Just as we have to let our children grow up, freeing them from our expectations, we also have to let them find their own ways of celebrating traditions. In the end, I discovered that it is kind of nice not to have to single-handedly cook a feast for thirty people. Taking those homemade pies they love over to their house is just as much fun.

> Just as we have to let our children grow up, freeing them from our expectations, we also have to let [adult children] find their own ways of celebrating traditions.

Then there are those conflicted holidays. Easter seems pretty straightforward, except for that blasted bunny, and of course, the ever-confusing Halloween. Is it a Christian holiday celebrating those who have died before us or a demonic death watch? It is very easy to start swatting at gnats and swallowing camels. I spent many years swatting only to feel that maybe dressing up was okay since it was just so much fun. We had originally stopped celebrating Halloween, substituting Reformation Day, when our second son got frightened of scary Halloween costumes at the door. We also had to stop going to Fourth of July fireworks with this timid child. You would laugh if I told you what he grew up to be. Nobody would call him timid today.

Since we decided Halloween was too scary for our young children, we also quickly decided to glorify our decision as spiritually superior. We kept up this stance until our youngest child reached about six. New to our neighborhood, we discovered that our new elderly neighbors waited all evening for the boys to trick-or-treat. Suddenly, with no little ones to be concerned about and living in a lovely neighborhood full of elderly people, Halloween seemed like a way to make other people happy. So Andrew and Alex grew up trick-or-treating, and Alex even came up with a system with a neighbor boy to change costumes in order to bank some extra candy. Alex even got to go trick-or-treating with his little nieces a couple of times.

During the years we shunned Halloween, we still had quite a bit of fun celebrating Reformation Day. The kids would dress up as their favorite reformer. Timothy once pretended to lay an egg in order to be Erasmus, the man that laid the egg that Luther hatched, so-to-speak. The children would give reports or recitations. We ate chili and had an all-round good time, sometimes even celebrating with our church family.

For Easter, we went through similar machinations. No Easter egg hunt for years, not because they were scary, but because the Easter Bunny seemed like an aberration (and it still does). Still, we ended up deciding an egg hunt was not so much of an aberration. We dyed one egg deep red to represent the blood of Christ, a tradition picked up from our Greek neighbors, and we went full speed ahead with extreme Rollins family competition, complete with chocolate crosses for prizes. I do so wonder about myself sometimes.

Decorating our homes for the changing seasons and coming holidays is part of the art of homemaking. Our doorsteps can welcome guests with pumpkins and wreaths. It is refreshing to decorate, and it is equally as refreshing to vacuum up all those pine needles (it would be a tad more absurd to have a fake tree, right?) and return to normalcy. Without holidays we wouldn't be able to bear the routines of our healthy daily habits. God is so good to acknowledge this need and to allow us to creatively greet each new season and holiday with our own unique palettes and traditions. Some of us think one day is special, and others think another day is special (seriously, I could care less about Valentine's Day), but let each of us celebrate as fully and as beautifully as we can, for the day is passing, and we know not what tomorrow brings.

Music in the Home

John Hodges tells us that to be truly educated one must know a few key things: the plays of Shakespeare, the paintings of Rembrandt, and Bach's *Mass in B Minor*.[3] That is not too hard is it? At least not at first glance. But as we get into the teleology of any of these things, we find that the very reason they are so worthy is that they run deep.

Music is a central part of our lives, and learning to love it generally comes easy to us. Learning to love what we should love is often quite a bit harder. It is easier to listen to pop music than classical music. Even though now it is easier than ever before to access the world's greatest music, we often don't even know where to start. I usually just say, "Alexa, play Bach's *Mass in B Minor*," or "Alexa, play *St. Matthew Passion*." Can you imagine how important concerts were to people of the past with no radios, record players, or Spotify?

Years ago we collected classical CDs and fell in love with a few of them. *Vivaldi for Lovers* was one, and *Music for a Sunny Sunday* was another. You don't need children at home to use AmblesideOnline's terms for composer study, or any other study for that matter. Concentrating for a month or more on one composer can go a long way in sealing his or her works in your mind. The Great Courses by The Teaching Company has many excellent lectures on classical music.[4] Try the lectures of Robert Greenberg. National Public Radio also has several informative programs on classical music.

Beyond classical music there is another category of neglected music in our time—hymns. David Powlison's book *God's Grace in Your Suffering* is crafted around the great hymns of the faith that speak to us in our suffering. The nicest thing about hymns was (and I say "was," as they do seem to be passing away) that they connected one generation to the next through the common culture of music. Hymns also are mini-teaching moments that draw us closer to God with age-old truths. If you don't sing hymns in your church, you might want to find a few hymns to sing to yourself during the week. I love much of the new Christian music, but there is something about "It Is Well with My Soul" that is unsurpassed. My dad loved the hymn "Great Is Thy Faithfulness" because it was written from a place of pain. And who can forget that, on the night before they died, Jim Elliot, Nate Saint, Ed McCully, Peter Fleming, and Roger Youderian sang *a capella* on the beach to the haunting tune of Finlandia, "Be Still my Soul."

Hobbies

Having a hobby is perhaps the definition of joyful creating. Our hobbies are things we choose. Hobbies may require intensity and hard work, time and money, but these are things we choose to spend our resources on. Our hobbies are by their very natures chosen. For some women, as we have discussed, their hobby is learning. They study as a hobby. Other women are more artistic, they create beautiful items from wool, cloth, or thread. Very often hobbies turn into small businesses, but that can also be lethal to the unhindered joy hobbies bring us. Still, it is gratifying when others appreciate what we have created and want to pay us for our time and effort. But our hobbies do not depend on this appreciation; they just depend on love.

Some years there will be few spare hours and few hobbies.

Our minds are always searching for mental nourishment to fill the spare hours. Some years there will be few spare hours and few hobbies. Other times we will fill the gaps created by change with things we love to do. Various hobbies have come and gone from my life over the years. In the early years of my marriage, I spent a lot of time cross-stitching. Even though I haven't touched a project in years, I still carry my case of threads from home to home. Those colorful strands remind me of someone I used to know: me. I made running a hobby for a while after my oldest children began leaving the nest. I was pleasantly surprised to find that suddenly I had more time on my hands. For a few years, I knitted. I often consider returning to that hobby. I imagine knitting as a way to make use of time spent binging on British TV. I suppose my hobby these days is writing. I am energized when I sit at my computer writing and thinking.

Some people make a hobby of collecting things, and I am always happy to buy a gift for a person like that. It is easy to get it right—roosters or tea cups or seashells. So easy for the gift-giver.

I used to collect children's books, but then I gave them away to my own children. It was gratifying to visit both my grandchildren and my old books at my oldest son's house recently. Which reminds me, grandchildren can be a sort of hobby.

My husband makes cutting boards as a hobby. It could become a business, only if it does, I will have to kill him. Last time that happened, our whole house became a wood shop and our children wood elves. Still, his cutting boards are incredibly finished and beautiful. He really can't ask people to pay what they are worth, so they make a better hobby.

The small things we do for love really are the things that last.

I like it when our hobbies make our homes, our places, more beautiful. Even decorating can be a hobby. Some girls know just how to place a pillow, and some girls know how to make one. In my living room I have two special pieces of art—a painting of a ship and a wooden trunk—made by my grandfather, my children's great-grandfather and my grandchildren's great-great-grandfather. I am so happy my grandfather had a hobby—or three. His hobbies are what still keep me connected to him even though he died over forty years ago. The small things we do for love really are the things that last.

Hospitality

All of this talk of the home as a palette reminds us that we are not just creating for our own gratification, although we do get that as a gift. We are first creating a nest for our own families, but as we eventually find out, nestlings turn into fledglings and then fly away. Our nests are for far more than just our own families. They are places of hospitality. Places where we invite others in and make our place their place for a while. Whether we offer our guests a full feast or just a cup of water, we offer what we have.

For some of us this will come easier than for others. It will even be easier in some seasons than others. When our son James was home, it seemed we were the most hospitable people on Earth. When he moved away to college, we looked up one day and thought, "Where are all of our friends?" James was such a good friend, we had let him do all the work. We had to start again learning how to invite people in. Right now, I am in a dry period of hospitality. Caring for my elderly mother has kept me from being able to have people over as much. Every once in a while we light up the bonfire and call people over spontaneously. We have even taken to offering our bonfire spot for other friends and groups from church to use when we are not home. I look forward to the days when we can once again have people over for meals, even if I just buy the food from a local restaurant. That's okay too. The important thing is to open our hearts and homes. One of my favorite books on hospitality is by Karen Mains titled *Open Heart, Open Home*. Karen reminds us that we are not entertaining our guests.

> Secular entertaining is a terrible bondage. Its source is human pride. Demanding perfection, fostering the urge to impress, it is a rigorous taskmaster which enslaves. In contrast, Scriptural hospitality is a freedom which liberates.[5]

When we have people over, we are not trying to show off our latest farmhouse decor piece or our farm fresh table; we are opening our hearts to hear their stories—not necessarily tell ours.

If you are creating a home, why not share it?

I can't help but think about how many Old Testament Bible stories are based on a lack of hospitality, some with horrific results. The *Odyssey* by Homer is considered a manual of Greek hospitality. It taught the Greeks the culture of how to treat a stranger. My neighbors hosted a young man in their home for a whole year while he completed a fellowship, even though they are in the midst of the most intense years of child-raising. They are a young family, but I want to be like Rachel and Nate, opening my home when it is not completely convenient. If we wait until things are perfect, it will never happen. If you are creating a home, why not share it?

A Woman I Know: Jody Combs

I have to admit that whenever I visit my sister's home I am a little bit jealous. She doesn't have a lot of money, but somehow she makes her whole home look put-together and decorated. She works really hard at this, but then again so do I without half the success. After visiting her, I usually come home and try again to make a room look decorated. Her creative energies used in her home make it seem inviting and comfortable.

My sister and I started out as quite different people. When she was twelve, if I went in her room while she was at school, used her brush on my hair, and placed it down on the dresser again, when she arrived home, she tore through the house asking, "Who moved my brush?" But then she grew up and had children, and of course, that pretty much cured her; but still her house is always clean. Cleaner than mine. While I was reading books about philosophy, she was reading books about having a lovely home, and it shows. But even though we started out so different from one another, sometimes she talks to me about what I am reading, or we even read a book together, and sometimes I imitate how she decorates her house. We complement each other very well and learn from one another.

My sister is also an excellent southern cook. While I am a pretty good cook when I feel like it, which is getting rarer and rarer, she always puts on a great table for her family and their many, many guests. In the end, having a comfortable home and comfortable food is about hospitality, and my sister is undaunted by the large crowds of basketball players she is often called on to feed and sometimes mother. Her gifts seem to be practical, but in the end she uses them for spiritual gain. She isn't just a Martha fretting in the kitchen while Mary basks at Jesus's feet. Jody is a Martha/Mary combo of hospitality. She doesn't need to read books about hospitality, she needs to write one.

The Ideal and the Reality

Here again we find ourselves up against our own romantic notions and the realities of being vulnerable. To create a home and then to open our home to others is to make ourselves vulnerable. After all, people have different tastes. And let's be honest, some of us feel threatened by the talents and skills of others. I have felt that way with my sister before, and she has felt that way with me. Sometimes we have what I call reverse snobbery. We feel more comfortable in someone's messy house than someone's pristine one, when really we should be accepting of both. If someone opens their home to us, we should accept it as a great gift and not quibble if they ask us to take off our shoes, nor if the kitchen floor looks like toddlers mopped it. To visit in another's home can sometimes bring awkward moments—like when the dog won't stop smelling you, or you step on a Lego. As with all of life, there is a balance to making people feel comfortable. I laughed myself silly at the online video of a family getting ready for guests with mom screaming orders. My mom taught me the age old trick of running around like a crazy person cleaning the house before company arrives. Once, I finally got the nerve to be a little more chill about company coming. That was a disaster too. A snobby lady came that day and made sure I knew her standards had been violated. I swore I would never be chill again. But sometimes people just drop by, or at least they used to in the olden days. To be welcoming is far more important than to have it all together.

> If someone opens their home to us, we should accept it as a great gift.

There are limits to how far we can take our creativity too. For most of us, our budgets limit our ability to make our home a Pinterest showcase. Stay within your budget. That is the road to happiness. You can spend a lot of money on unsuccessful Pinterest projects if you are me, but if you are my sister, they might turn out after all. Know yourself. When we are secure in Christ, we can afford to revel in the gifts and talents and budgets of others.

Suggested Reading

The Hidden Art of Homemaking by Edith Schaeffer

The Mind of the Maker by Dorothy L. Sayers

Inheriting Paradise: Meditations on the Art of Gardening by Vigen Guroian

Open Heart, Open Home by Karen Mains

Real Love for Real Life: The Art and Work of Caring by Andi Ashworth

Hallelujah: Cultivating Advent Traditions with Handel's Messiah by Cindy Rollins

Waiting on the Word by Malcolm Guite

The Supper of the Lamb by Robert Farrar Capon

Favorite Cookbooks

Betty Crocker's Cooky Book by Betty Crocker

The Pioneer Woman Cooks by Ree Drummond (and others by the author)

Nourishing Traditions: The Cookbook that Challenges Politically Correct Nutrition by Sally Fallon, Mary G. Enig and Marion Dearth

Growth Ideas

- Invite someone over to dinner.
- Have an informal fire pit gathering.
- Try a new recipe from a real cookbook.
- Make something for your family that your grand-mother made for you.

CHAPTER EIGHT

The Beautiful Mother

I believe happy girls are the prettiest girls.

Audrey Hepburn

Inner Beauty

We live in an age of images. I admit that I am more of a word person than an image one. I like pretty pictures as much as the next person, but Instagram leaves me feeling hollow, as if everything were really just a hologram. Words seem more solid. That is just me; I know that. But this age of images has left us scrambling around for new definitions of beauty. Inner beauty is something you cannot see, and as a result it cannot possibly be as important as outer beauty in an age of images. Nevertheless, inner beauty is real. We all know someone who seems unattractive until we have gotten to know them, and then we cannot remember why we felt that way. In contrast, I have met drop-dead gorgeous women whose beauty fades the minute they open their mouths.

Even so, in an age of images we all want to be outwardly thin, fit, and beautiful. We are willing to buy whatever it takes to make ourselves that way. Sometimes we are willing to put our consciences aside to buy questionable products from questionable sources to chase after outward and fleeting beauty. I have heard that in some communities women in their twenties are opting for plastic surgery and injections of all sorts to keep their skin completely smooth. Our very looks are changing along with our values. A virtuous woman who can find? Do we even care? Celebrity women older than me, such as Sally Field and Jane Fonda, now look younger than me. And plastic surgery is getting better and better. They do not have the permanent surprised look on their faces of last year's model. I can sit here and scoff, but I am not entirely sure that if I had enough money and enough friends doing these things I would not do them myself. I am not sure.

And yet the Bible says that charm is deceitful and beauty is vain. This must be true because God did not create us all physically attractive. It seems almost unfair in this Instagram world for God to make some of us less than pretty, but He did. Quite obviously, He has a different way of seeing than we do. And He tells us this in His Word, "Man looks at the outward appearance, but God looks at the heart."[1]

Proverbs 11:22 says, "Like a gold ring in a pig's snout is a beautiful woman without discretion." Here we begin to see what inner beauty might look like. A woman with inner beauty will have discretion. The first definition of discretion is "the quality of behaving or speaking in such a way as to avoid causing offense or revealing private information."[2] That short definition alone is enough for contemplation. A discrete woman is a beautiful woman. This often comes down to our feelings of insecurity and inferiority. We are often indiscreet when we feel badly about ourselves and are seeking affirmation. A confident, warm woman can afford to be discrete. She doesn't have a chip on her shoulder. Maybe inner beauty doesn't always translate to outer beauty, but it can help us rest in confidence that to the true King we are all glorious.

Recently, it has come home to me just how important it is for a mother in her home, a mother who has chosen to be in her home, a mother who has chosen to homeschool, to make sure her children see her smile. If you want to have a happy home, you are going to have to start with a happy face. I tended to think of myself as a happy person while I was raising my children. I enjoyed it so much, and yet I suspect now if you asked my children, they might not have gotten this message, especially my middle children. I think I got so caught up in the seriousness of it all that I forgot to show my inner joy. For truly, I felt inner joy almost every day. I never had trouble getting out of bed in the morning. But did I smile? I think there are so many sad things that might have never happened if I would have just smiled. Smiling is one of the key elements of beauty. Audrey Hepburn herself, that paragon of inner and outer beauty, said, "I believe happy girls are the prettiest girls." Charlotte Mason said something similar, "We all know how the physical effort of smiling affects ourselves in our sour moods." She said this long before modern brain research found that we can control our emotions with our face.

> If you want to have a happy home, you are going to have to start with a happy face.

Here in our modern times, we don't generally find value in faking emotions we do not feel. We search for authenticity and wear it like a badge of honor. We air our dirty laundry because that feels more real than hiding it. While I appreciate this generation's pursuit of authenticity, I am afraid that both hiding our emotions and displaying them for all to see are not truly the definition of authenticity. Modern counselors do not like the old fake-it-till-you-make-it advice, and I get that. It can be destructive if not understood properly. But C. S. Lewis reminds us in *Mere Christianity:*

> The rule for all of us is perfectly simple. Do not waste time bothering whether you "love" your neighbor; act as if you did. As soon as we do this we find one of the great secrets. When you are behaving as if you loved someone, you will presently come to love him . . . There is, indeed, one exception. If you do him a good turn, not to please God and obey the law of charity, but to show him what a fine forgiving chap you are, and to put him in your debt, and then sit down to wait for his "gratitude," you will probably be disappointed.[3]

If we love our children, then we will make sure they see that by our smiles. I don't think inner beauty is a gift like outer beauty is. I think it must be cultivated. A good place to start cultivating inner beauty is by applying Charlotte Mason's motto to ourselves rather than just our children: I am, I can, I ought, I will.

Listening

We live in a noisy world. We can hardly keep up with all the content, podcasts, ideas, lesson plans, and pictures coming our way. I used to wonder why people came up to talk to me after I gave a talk. What did they want from me? I was happy to talk to them, but I felt drained and wasn't sure how to give them more. Then I realized they didn't want to listen to me more, they wanted me to listen to them, something I could very easily do. I could listen to them, hear them, and pray for them even when I could not physically help them. Listening is a lost art. We are programmed by modernity to want to feed each other content. When we stop to listen, it can be a wonderful break. It is a way of giving that gives rest to the giver.

I have not always been a good listener. I got in the habit of teaching my children and that turned into the habit of talking at them. One of my regrets is that I did not listen more. I am trying hard now to stop talking (they have heard enough of me) and start listening. It is gratifying to hear about who they are and what they are doing. I feel privileged when they share this, and it becomes a treasure in my heart. It also helps me pray for them when I wake up in the wee hours of the morning and can't sleep. It is my goal to speak the names of each of my family members before the throne of God each day. Listening to my children helps me do that well.

One of the ways we signal that we are listening is by making eye contact. One of my parents thought that making eye contact with people was dangerous and even wrong. This idea affected my childhood and my life deeply. It has taken me years to look someone in the eye when they are speaking to me. It has been awkward and frustrating but worth the effort. I have to practice listening and practice making eye contact. Something so seemingly simple takes massive effort on my part, and yours, I suspect. The key to listening to people is not being afraid of the silences. I am a notorious

> It is my goal to speak the names of each of my family members before the throne of God each day.

silence filler. When the room gets quiet, I feel it is my responsibility to fix it. This is one reason why I was a bad listener. Learning to be comfortable with the silences of conversation is also hard work. While listening seems like a passive activity, it is really a gargantuan task. But it is a task which reaps great rewards. By listening, we begin to learn about other people, and that helps us in life. It helps us make connections, and it helps us see patterns; skills we need to effectively communicate with one another.

Mothers are generous human beings who would do almost anything for their offspring. Learning to listen is one of the ways they can cultivate beauty in their homes and relationships. It is just so easy not to notice that we don't listen when we are barking out orders and setting up efficient ways to run our families.

Besides listening to our children and to those we want to love and minister to, we can also learn to listen to God. Learning to see is the art of attention. Learning to listen is also part of this art. When we learn to listen to God, we begin to hear His voice in all we do. Meditation is one way to learn to listen to God. I don't like to think of it as emptying my mind—completely leaving it open to evil as well as good. I like to think of it as opening my mind to the spiritual world where we really live and move and have our being. When we begin to listen to God, when we stop talking to Him and let Him talk to us, the universe aligns. Sorrows and joys begin to make sense. When we listen to God, we begin to see and understand how He works, which is not at all the way we go about things.

> Learning to listen is one of the ways [moms] can cultivate beauty in their homes and relationships.

Sometimes the world gets even noisier than usual. This week is one of those weeks. It seems that everyone I know has an opinion. I have tried to listen to their opinions, but the noise is so loud I have decided I need to stop listening to the world and start listening to the silence. Not everything is worthy of our ear.

As I write this, I sit on my porch. I can hear the breeze through the branches of the trees, the call of bird upon bird upon bird, the crackling of the leaves as an animal scurries across the ground, the twirl of a leaf falling to the ground, and the tap-tapping of Max's toenails as he wonders how long we are going to sit here. Ouch, there was a car passing. In that car were people with Facebook pages and opinions. Today I cannot listen to them and continue to be human. Today I must keep silent. I must not add to the cacophony, but I must not listen either because it will break me.

> We need to listen to something altogether outside of ourselves.

They say that our nation is polarized and that the cure is to listen better to one another. I doubt that. I have tried that, and it doesn't make me like the people I disagree with more nor even the ones I agree with. We don't need to listen more to one another in the public sphere. We need to listen to something altogether outside of ourselves.

We spoke in earlier chapters of the beginning of wisdom being at the place of "I don't know." Listening is one of the greatest tools for learning that we have available to us. We just have to know what to listen to.

"Hear, O Israel: The LORD our God, the LORD is one" (Deut. 6:4). That's a start. That's the beginning.

Friendship

One of the things I learned by writing my book *Mere Motherhood* is that a memoir makes for a lot of friends. So many women told me they felt like my friend, like they knew me already. That was gratifying and scary. Scary because something in me wants to be deep and real with all of them, and of course, that is impossible.

Friendship is an important part of feminine identity. Women make wonderful friends and terrible enemies. As Rudyard Kipling says, "The female of the species is more deadly than the male."[4] Most of what I have learned in life has come from my friends, especially if you consider books as friends, like I do.

Along the way I have collected many beautiful friends, most of them smarter than me. My long-term friendships have been born from women I met amongst newsletter subscribers (I guess that was our pre-Instagram community) and email lists. I have now known a whole group of longtime homeschooling classical educators for over twenty years. I still sit at their feet and learn, process it through my own experiences, and turn around and share with you. If you don't like what I say, blame them.

When I was young, I was sometimes lonely. I liked being alone but that did not make for friendship building. With the birth of the internet, introverts finally had a way to develop friendships. Women's friendships can be tricky. We talk about a sisterhood, but we often feel threatened and competitive with one another. We compare ourselves to each other. We despise the prettiest woman or the thinnest woman or the woman with the floor you can eat off of. We can fall into gossip easily to cover our insecurities. We are fierce and emotional about our children. All of these things can hijack our friendships with one another, and yet we constantly crave someone to talk to over the back fence.

I miss those days even though I hardly knew them. I imagine my mother hanging out the wash on the line, the breeze flapping through the sheets as she heads over to have coffee and a Danish with her next door neighbor. I had that once, but it was with a much older woman. She came over to my house each day with tea and cookies. I was swamped with small children, but she came to me. She shared with me secrets of life I have never forgotten—some so personal I would never share here, but tips and hints that have helped me live the thirty years which have passed since we spent those sweet afternoons together. I listened to her and she, bless her heart, listened to my young, opinionated self. Now I know what grace looks like. She was gracious to me when I must have seemed very silly to her.

> I need friends who will love me even if it takes nine months to meet for our monthly lunch . . .

A lifelong friendship is not unlike a marriage. It takes grace to stay friends with someone with faults and differences. My favorite friendships are low maintenance. I need friends who will love me even if it takes nine months to meet for our monthly lunch and thankfully, I have them.

Our longtime friends are the ones who can be the iron that sharpens our iron. We desperately need to be sharpened and loved at the same time. It is easy to sharpen an enemy, but love makes it hard to confront our friends, that is why those confrontations are so precious. Our old friends can stand to be patient with us as we struggle to hear what they are saying. We can't dismiss them as not understanding so easily. The wounds of a friend are faithful indeed.

Mothers and Daughters

There is a unique kind of friendship in the life of a mother, and that is the relationship between a mother and an adult daughter. In my experience, this is not the easiest relationship. It is fraught with pitfalls and misunderstandings. It is hard for daughters to understand their mothers. I have never completely understood my own mother. I think this is complicated by knowing a lot about our mothers while at the same time knowing very little. Mothers and daughters are alike in so many ways, but then they are different too. My daughter did not want to be me any more than I wanted to be my mother. We want to differentiate ourselves from the women we are closest to. This makes navigating the relationship complex. But just like a marriage, these relationships are permanent, even when we don't act like they are. I cannot change who my mother is, so I can either honor her as the Bible suggests or reject her as unworthy. Over the years I have done a little of both, not because my mother is a monster deserving to be rejected, but because I have not always understood her, nor she me. As my mother's health declines, and she faces the hardship of dementia slowly stealing her mind, my rejection more often turns to honor. Even when I disagree with her, like the time she hitchhiked to go see my dad, I can still try to honor her as a woman in a stage of

I think this is complicated by knowing a lot about our mothers while at the same time knowing very little.

grief I have yet to experience. On some days I do this well, and on other days I simply lose my temper.

I have a dream image of what it would be like to have a happy relationship with my own daughter. In my dream, we laugh (my daughter has the best sense of humor) and shop and eat. She introduces me to her children, and I care for them and love them. We call each other on the phone (something in real life neither my daughter nor I enjoy), or maybe we just text one another daily. The pains and sorrows and hurts of the past are blunted by the joys of the present and the future. That is my dream. That is what God has given some of you, and I hope you thank Him and appreciate that gift. God has given me this kind of relationship with many young women, but for many years not with my own daughter. The hurts were too deep.

> These hard well-meaning hands we thrust
> Among the heart-strings of a friend.[5]

And then one day, I reached out to my daughter, and she answered my text. Since that day, my dream of going to Target and shopping with my daughter materialized, even though I feared it never would. We even went to Switzerland together, and just today she asked if I wanted to go white-water rafting with her soon. Would I?!

Often the most difficult feminine relationships in a woman's life are among those closest to her. Young women have to deal with the ups and downs of monthly cycles. Older woman get to go through what I can only say is a second puberty called menopause. We bring those ups and downs to our relationships. I am generally pretty chill. When I went through menopause, which I didn't realize I was going through at the time, I felt tremendously angry and emotionally unstable for a couple of years. Suddenly, one day I stopped crying and stopped feeling angry, and realized I had been through one of life's notorious upheavals. I haven't sobbed uncontrollably since then, and I am rarely upset. There's hormones for you. And they affect our emotions and our relationships because they affect the way we view our circumstances. This doesn't mean our perspectives aren't valid, only that wisdom requires we factor our hormonal state into how we judge our feelings or opinions.

Long term relationships deserve extra measures of grace. It is imperative that our children are connected to the generations that have come before, even when those generations are flawed and sinful. Without that connection, we are untethering our children into the future without a set of instructions they are going to need.

Mothers and daughters: it's complicated, but love is not so complicated. I simply love my daughter, and that is never going to stop. My love was not powerful enough to always keep her safe and unharmed, but it is powerful enough to wait for her forever.

Our Father's Daughters

> She will be led to the King in embroidered work;
> The virgins, her companions who follow her,
> Will be brought to You.
> They will be led forth with gladness and rejoicing;
> They will enter into the King's palace.
> (Psalm 45:14-15 NASB)

If you are a Christian, then you are the beautiful daughter of the greatest of Kings. Your beauty is a done deal. You are admired and loved, comforted and caressed by the King of Kings and Lord of Lords. What does it matter if your beauty is hidden? He sees.

In the world of women, we are quick to default to shallow values to hoist ourselves above the person next to us. But in the King's palace, we are fearfully and wonderfully made. We are constantly showered with blessings. When rebukes come, they bring healing, not more hurt. In the King's palace, we revel in joy, because we have been saved from ourselves, and we belong. We can live our lives in this palace, fearing no evil. Nothing can touch us apart from our Father's will. We can learn to be abased and to abound because nothing can separate us from the love of our Father the King.

> What does it matter if your beauty is hidden? He sees.

But fatherhood is also fraught with difficulties. Our earthly fathers are sinners. Our understanding of the fatherhood of God can be skewed by daddy issues. Take a minute to think about some TV show you watch. Are there daddy issues in that show? It sometimes seems that daddy issues are behind every single show on television. My old favorite TV show *Lost* told story after story of broken relationships between fathers and sons, and fathers and daughters.

It would almost seem like the enemy of us all has a vested interest in destroying our view of fatherhood. Psalm 27:10 reminds us that even when our mother and father forsake us, the Lord will take us up. It almost seems that God knew our earthly fathers would forsake us, let us down, hurt us, and He made a provision for that. If you are suffering because of daddy issues hear this:

> Listen, daughter, and pay careful attention:
> Forget your people and your father's house.
> Let the king be enthralled by your beauty;
> honor him, for he is your lord.
> (Psalm 45:10-11 NIV)

Followed up by this in verse 16:

> Your sons will take the place of your fathers;
> You will make them princes throughout the
> land. (NIV)

As a mother of sons, I have always loved that last verse.

Even the best earthly fathers let us down, because all have sinned and fall short of the glory of God. It is a sad fact, but it is a story with a happy ending. We have a father who sees us even as He saw the crying mother Hagar in the desert with her dying son, Ishmael. Someday, we shall know God as He already knows us.

A Woman I Knew: Lynn Bruce

It isn't easy to find women who are beautiful both inside and out, and yet it took me less than a second to decide who I would tell you about in this category. Lynn Bruce was a beautiful woman you didn't mind sharing space with. She never made you feel inferior. She was a genius at making other people feel important. I tend to be an imitator. Once, after spending a weekend with Lynn in a hotel room, she noticed this and said, "You do you." Why would I do me when I could imitate her? I often feel like I missed some of the instructions necessary to be womanly. That was why I watched and imitated Lynn. She did not miss that particular class. She knew how to be feminine, strong, and sassy. She was no shrinking violet, nor was she brassy and bossy. When I am in challenging situations I often ask myself, What would Lynn do? To just look at Lynn you might think that she had led a charmed life, and there was a time many, many years ago when I looked at her and thought, "That woman has it all." You might almost think that I was jealous. But now I know that Lynn did have it all. All the suffering and frustration that life can throw at a woman to knock her off of her game has been hers. Mercy. Courage. Grace. That is how she handled these increasing setbacks. Those are her words. Mercy. Courage. Grace. She looked at the giants in the land, but she didn't shrink back because she also knew that her Redeemer lives. Lynn wan't invincible, and she knew that more than anyone else, but she was a beautiful, beautiful woman both inside and out.

Today as I write, Lynn is even more beautiful that she was before. Lynn has gone on to be with the Lord, and while I miss her dreadfully every single day, I am so happy for her.

The Ideal and the Reality

Of all the ideals that confront us in modern life and on social media, none is more pervasive than the modern ideals of physical beauty. Recently, at a moms meeting, four older moms shared how they did it. Two of the moms were quite a bit older with many graduates, and two were just graduating their first children. Both of us older moms were a bit overweight, but the other two moms both spoke at length about how important working out was to them. As a consequence, they were both very attractive, but also driven. Chubby as I was, I could not help seeing something sad in their desperate efforts. In the couple of decades between me and these moms, the shift had changed from being slightly healthy to being obsessed with health and fitness. Not that there is anything wrong with being in shape and attractive—only it can become a goal that squeezes out all the joy in life. Once again we land right back at "everything in moderation." As older women, we could have afforded to think more about ourselves and our weight along the way, as younger women they might have afforded themselves a little breathing room.

As our visual world careens towards *Hunger Games*-absurdity in physical appearances, we would do well to remember that God clearly tells us that it is not our outward appearance that matters to Him. Physical discipline, while having some benefit, is not the source of value of the soul, and it is not what goes into the body that defiles it, but what comes out.

If you want authenticity, you are going to have to look for it outside of social media.

In the midst of all of this, there is the counter movement that searches for authenticity but fails to find it. Just because I show you a picture of me without makeup, doesn't mean I am now authentic. Authenticity is more than fat people in bikinis disrespecting themselves publicly. Authenticity happens in relationships. I don't have a real relationship with my Instagram followers, no matter how much I like their pretty pictures. I didn't write all my dirty laundry out in the pages of this book, but some of you know all about it because we have a relationship, and I can talk to you one-on-one. If you want authenticity, you are going to have to look for it outside of social media. It is the old notion that an audience always changes things. Authenticity is what happens behind the curtain of publicity. Publicity is anything we do on social media. Social media is a great place to meet people and test the waters, but if we want to be truly authentic, we have to meet in real life or at least correspond outside of the public eye.

Over the years, I have met many beautiful women, most of them only beautiful on the outside after I have gotten to know their insides. Once you see the beauty a woman possesses inside, it is hard to forget. It is hard to ever think of them as unattractive again. Some women are physically beautiful in a way that causes everyone who sees them to admire them. This is a special gift, but it is not the best gift. I am told a beautiful woman has nowhere to hide. All eyes are upon her, male and female. Some eyes crave her and some despise her, but very few just accept her beauty as a gift.

So there we have it. Some of us are beautiful inside and some outside, and a few are beautiful inside and outside. The Bible says it is the hidden beauty of the heart that matters most. Which makes me think we had better be careful about how we judge one another. We might not know what is hidden. We might not see that we are hurting one of God's favored ones.

Suggested Reading

Boundaries by Dr. Henry Cloud and Dr. John Townsend

CHAPTER NINE

The Suffering Mother

> Beloved, do not think it strange concerning the fiery
> trial which is to try you, as though some strange thing
> happened to you; but rejoice to the extent that you
> partake of Christ's sufferings, that when His glory is
> revealed, you may also be glad with exceeding joy.
>
> I Peter 4:12-14 (NKJV)

The Inevitable

I didn't really want to write this chapter. Nor live it. But I think of all who have shared their suffering with me and how much that comforted me—I was not alone.

If you are alive, you are going to suffer at times in your life. If you are a parent, you signed up for a certain amount of suffering. To have hopes and dreams is to invite pain and disappointment. To have hopes and dreams for others is even more risky. In many ways, to love is to suffer. Elisabeth Elliot observes:

> Let's never forget that if we don't ever want to suffer, we must be very careful never to love anything or anybody. The gifts of love have been the gifts of suffering. Those two things are inseparable.[1]

This from a woman who lost two husbands.

Since my father died, my mother, who also suffers some dementia, keeps saying, "I wish I hadn't married someone five years older than me." As if marrying someone the same age would have guaranteed a different outcome. Her love of over sixty years made her grief seem unbearable. We are reminded that if our hope is only for this life, we are indeed the most wretched people of all. Truly we should eat, drink, and be merry, and certainly not care about anyone or anything.

In some ways that is the modern answer. C. S. Lewis talks about this in *The Abolition of Man*. Humanity who has rejected God has only one answer to the problem of pain. Don't care. Lewis talks about ordering our loves, and not laughing at honor. If you want to avoid suffering, you are going to have to be careful not to care about anything. But there is a better way.

The very nature of suffering is pain, always emotional and often physical. Elisabeth Elliot defines suffering this way, "Suffering is having what you don't want or wanting what you don't have."[2] It often seems entirely random and without reason. Without the eyes of faith, suffering produces bitterness.

Once again, Elisabeth Elliot has the answer:

> You either believe God knows what He's doing or you believe He doesn't. You either believe He's worth trusting or you say He's not. And then, where are you? You're at the mercy of chaos not cosmos. *Chaos* is the Greek word for disorder. *Cosmos* is the word for order. We either live in an ordered universe or we are trying to create our own reality. [3]

From the moment we marry or become pregnant, we are opening our lives up to suffering, but many single people suffer loneliness—another form of pain. We cannot run from suffering. For humans there is nowhere to hide. Either our suffering has eternal purposes, or it is completely inexplicable and futile.

While it is easy to share our little disappointments in life, like our inability to keep our house clean or our children in line, it is much harder to share our real failure and our real suffering.

Joy and Suffering

Older moms have faced a lot of failure and suffering. Titus 2 comes with a price tag. If that were the end of the story, I would not be writing this book at all. For most of my Christian life, I struggled with the concept of joy. I knew I was supposed to feel it, possess it, but I couldn't honestly say that I did. Intellectually, I knew that a Christian is someone who has been forgiven and therefore the response to this great gift should be gratitude and joy. I sort of understood gratitude, even before modern technology turned it into cheesy pictures of Bibles and coffee mugs. It was somewhat easy to say "thank you" for the gift of salvation, but it was extremely difficult for me to feel the joy of the Lord. Instead, what I felt was constant frustration with my own failure and inadequacies as a Christian.

> We cannot run from suffering. For humans there is nowhere to hide.

Being a Christian seemed like a massive test in which I was always coming up short. Not real short, just enough to make me constantly frustrated with not being able to live up to my own high ideals. Being a Christian was a major downer. I wouldn't have said my theology involved my deserving salvation, but it certainly involved my living up to my salvation in some way.

And then one day I didn't. I didn't live up to my own ideals, which I based on my ideas about God. I failed, and I caused hurt and pain in other people. It was such a massive, unforeseen failure, I could not wiggle out of it. I could not justify it in any way. I had to live with it. Day in and day out, I had to live with the knowledge that I had caused irreparable hurt. This brought about deep suffering, in my own life and in the lives of others. I was like an animal thrashing in pain, trying to run away from it. When I lay my head on my pillow at night, I soaked it with my tears. For two years, I cried and thrashed and ran from the pain. But whenever I looked up, Christ was there. I could not escape Him. I began to be very aware that He loved me. I began to notice His gifts— the gifts I recorded earlier, like the moon and the stars. Suddenly, His gifts seemed to be everywhere. His gifts were delightful. His gifts brought me joy. And there I was in the midst of terrible anguish, feeling something that had eluded me for the whole of my Christian life—joy. The suffering hadn't created the joy; it had just stripped all the layers of me away enough so that I could see the joy.

One Sunday, our pastor spoke on the verse, "It is good for me that I have been afflicted" (Psalm 119:71a NKJV), and I got it. It was good. I didn't feel the need anymore to beg God to stop afflicting me because I knew that it was all love and that I didn't have to fear it anymore. I knew that whatever affliction came my way, and I also knew that it would come my way, it would continue to reveal truth and bring joy. Joy was mine. It was after I found joy that I was able to see that I could forgive myself, even if others didn't. If Christ forgave me, and I clearly saw that I belonged to him, then who was I to walk in unforgiveness towards myself or others? I didn't need the power to forgive myself because God already had that power. It was already mine in Christ. As Christ grew immeasurably bigger in my mind, none of my sins had the power to stand against him. He conquered my heart and my sin. I didn't have to go on being unhappy as some sort of penance. Nothing can separate us from the love of God in Christ Jesus. Not suffering and not sin. This should help us forgive those who have hurt us. Bitterness and unforgiveness can not compete with joy.

One of my sons suggested a book on the subject of joy by Mike Mason titled *Champagne for the Soul*. It was the last step I needed to take in the painful journey. It confirmed what I was beginning to suspect. I didn't have to deserve joy. It was just a gift. What started out as despair, pain, and suffering, ended with absolute trust and faith in Christ. I can do all things through Christ who strengthens me.

During the last few years, I have read many books on suffering. One of the key takeaways I have from this reading is that suffering leads to intimacy with God. A. W. Tozer is attributed with saying that "God doesn't have favorites, but He does have intimates." Suffering strips away the veil and allows us to see the face of God.

> I didn't have to deserve joy. It was just a gift.

Another book I read on suffering was *God's Grace in Your Suffering* by David A. Powlinson. The book was intimate and helpful, but on finishing it I learned that Mr. Powlinson had just been diagnosed with Stage 4 cancer. My first reaction was dismay. It hardly seemed fair that just because he wrote a book on suffering he should have to suffer more. And yet, the more I thought about what he wrote, the more I realized that he must be one of those intimates of God. Here is one of my favorite quotes from Powlinson's book:

> In other words, your significant sufferings don't happen by accident. There's no random chance. No purposeless misery. No bad luck. Not even (and understand this the right way) a tragedy. Tragedy means ruin, destruction, downfall, an unhappy ending with no redemption. Your life story may contain a great deal of misery and heartache along the way. But in the end, in Christ, your life story will prove to be a comedy in the original sense of the word, a story with a happy ending.[4]

As Christians, we cannot escape the happy ending no matter how far from our sight it is today.

The Art of Lament

God has not left us alone to come up with some sort of theology of suffering. In His Word, the Bible, He has given us a tool to use when we are suffering. It is "lament." It is quite remarkable in that it offers us a chance to whine, cry, gnash our teeth, and complain to God, and when we are done, it allows us to fall on our knees and worship. It is truly a significant tool for Christians everywhere. Interestingly, although I have been a Christian for over fifty years, I had never really heard of lament formally. My dad did often say that his favorite passage in the Bible was Lamentations 3. Here is part of it:

> I am the man who has seen affliction
>   under the rod of His wrath;
> he has driven and brought me
>   into darkness without any light;
> surely against me he turns his hand
>   again and again the whole day long.
>
> He has made my flesh and my skin waste away;
>   he has broken my bones;
> he has besieged and enveloped me
>   with bitterness and tribulation;
> he has made me dwell in darkness
>   like the dead of long ago.
>
> He has walled me about so that I cannot escape;
>   he has made my chains heavy;
> though I call and cry for help,
>   he shuts out my prayer;
> he has blocked my ways with blocks of stones;
>   he has made my paths crooked.
>
> He is a bear lying in wait for me,
>   a lion in hiding;
> he turned aside my steps and tore me to pieces;
>   he has made me desolate;

he bent his bow and set me
    as a target for his arrow.

He drove into my kidneys
    the arrows of his quiver;
I have become the laughingstock of all peoples,
    the object of their taunts all day long.
he has filled me with bitterness;
    he has sated me with wormwood.

He has made my teeth grind on gravel,
    and made me cower in ashes;
my soul is bereft of peace;
    I have forgotten what happiness is;
so I say, "My endurance has perished;
    so has my hope from the LORD."

Remember my affliction and my wanderings,
    the wormwood and the gall!
My soul continually remembers it
    and is bowed down within me
But this I call to mind,
    and therefore I have hope:

The steadfast love of the LORD never ceases;
    His mercies never come to an end;
they are new every morning;
    great is your faithfulness.
"The LORD is my portion," says my soul,
    "therefore I will hope in him."

Here we find Jeremiah, the man of constant sorrow, in the pit, a literal cistern, alone and dying. And here we find one of the greatest affirmations of faith in the Bible:

> The steadfast love of the Lord never ceases;
>> his mercies never come to an end;
> they are new every morning;
>> great is your faithfulness.

I'm sure you can guess what my dad's favorite hymn was.

> Great is Thy faithfulness, O God my Father;
> there is no shadow of turning with Thee;
> Thou changest not, Thy compassions, they fail not;
> as Thou hast been, Thou forever wilt be.

> Great is Thy faithfulness!
> Great is Thy faithfulness!
> Morning by morning new mercies I see;
> all I have needed Thy hand hath provided:
> great is Thy faithfulness, Lord, unto me!

We sang that at his funeral. Whenever anyone asks me my favorite hymn for any service or banquet, I always respond, "Great Is Thy Faithfulness." A lament from the pit.

There are a lot of interesting things that scholars tell us about lament. Many laments are chiasms in their structure. A chiasm is shaped like the letter X, meaning that the ideas are presented in a sequence until the main idea is expressed, and then the ideas are repeated in reverse order. The most important element forms the hinge point of the structure. So an idea is presented, often a complaint, then it builds to a praise and then it offers more praise as it returns to sorrow.

Everything about lament is edgy. It is God allowing us the space to have emotions but reminding us that those emotions are not the whole story. Mark Vroegop, in his book *Dark Clouds, Deep Mercy,* says that even Jesus lamented on the cross.

> Jesus quoted Psalm 22:1, "Why have you forsaken me?" on the cross. In other words, Jesus lived a life of lament. He knows the sorrows of injustice, hypocrisy, false accusations, physical weakness, temptations, betrayal, and feeling abandoned. That becomes the basis for our bold requests.[5]

In every way He was tempted like us YET without sin. Lament, to be effective, must be humble. It must acknowledge that we cannot see everything but that in our sorrow we believe. "Lament stands in the gap between pain and promise."[6]

Lament in Real Life

I love the name the British use for a certain type of (dysfunctional) family life. They call it "playing happy families." Doesn't that hit at the root of everything we want? We want a happy family. That is not a bad desire. But it includes a million things outside of our control, hence the name of the game implying that "happy families" is only something we can pretend.

To be honest, that really is good news once you get used to it. We can work on the things that we do have control over and leave the other things in better hands.

I was talking to my friend Jeannette Tulis recently, and she told me about a conversation she had with Elisabeth Elliot. Jeannette asked Elisabeth, "Is it safe to hope?" I love Elisabeth's answer.

> It is safe to hope in what we long for, for we hope as a child with a good Father, we hope knowing He will give us His best, we come to Him honestly with our hopes knowing He knows us, all our circumstances, and will take our hopes and can change us. Give us His perspective as we pray, as we are faithful and work. But in the meantime HOPE.[7]

I have learned over sixty years that this true. I have seen God take some of my disordered hopes and redeem them. It is like He is letting me know that He SEES me. And not just once. Over and over again in this life, sometimes years later, God shows me that He saw.

When I wrote *Mere Motherhood,* things were going downhill in my family. It was like one day everything seemed good and the next day, well, you know, Mad Max territory. As I finished up the prologue (the last part of the book I wrote), things began to turn around, but then suddenly after the book was released things took another nose dive. For six years things were hard in our family, and yet I can truly say that I KNOW that my Redeemer lives. I can truly say that HE is better than ten sons. I can truly say that it was good for me that I was afflicted, and that I know now that I would choose Jesus over my family. Why? Because I can trust my family to Him.

A friend and I were talking this week, and she said, "Thank you so much for saying that communication isn't always the answer to family problems." This is something I have been known to say publicly. Here is the deal. Homeschooling mothers are very, very close to their children. It is a natural and beautiful thing, but there comes a time when we have to let our children go. My ears really perked up when a recent *Call the Midwife* episode began with this: "Abandonment is the successful parent's lot." I didn't know that when I was young, although maybe that is how it should be.

> Communication isn't always the answer to family problems.

Sometimes we know people, or we see pictures of large, happy families living in proximity to one another, and we long for that closeness. Then our children grow up and take a natural step of walking away from us, their mothers. Sometimes homeschooled kids have to do this more violently to just to go through a natural process. This about rips mom's heart out. It really isn't against her, although it may look and feel that way for awhile.

Older moms or middle moms face the unthinkable. Their children are growing up and away, and it hurts.

But younger moms are facing something else. In a way, they themselves are growing up and away from their own parents.

Sometimes young moms can't see that the way they treat their parents now will one day be the way their children treat them. Young moms seem to get so mad at their parents (sometimes for legitimate reasons and sometimes for not-so-legitimate reasons). Young moms, who are now so close to their small children, cannot imagine that happening between their children and themselves.

But it will. Which is why I believe the Bible says that we are to honor our parents. If you aren't honoring your parents for whatever reason, I would pray about how to go about that. For some it will be a much harder ordeal and may include setting a ton of boundaries. But it will help you when the time comes for your own children to grow up and grow apart from you.

In my case, my daughter grew away for six long years. Years that I probably mourned every single day. Years where I grew healthier in my self and relationship to Christ. Years where I let go of everything. And then one day I texted my daughter for the umpteenth time not even knowing if her phone number was the same, and she texted back.

When you sign up for parenthood, you sign up for a crash course in sanctification and humility and unconditional love. You sign up for not always knowing what to do and for making some big mistakes. You sign up for a great program that will show you that you can't do anything without Christ. It is a brash, rash, crazy, wonderful thing that throws you right where you need to be—on the mercy of Christ.

We fall short as parents because we are sinners. The wages of sin is death, BUT the good news is that Christ makes up the deficit. That is the whole Gospel. I remember an old illustration about swimmers swimming from California to Hawaii. Some were the best swimmers in the world and some were the worst, but none made it to Hawaii.

When I reflect back over my years of parenting, I see that the mistakes I made were often the things I thought at the time were good and wise, like teaching my daughter to be so modest she thought all lust was her fault. And the things I did right were almost accidental things.

I really, really do wish I had inspected more. Because that is tied to habits. I might have been waxing eloquently on honor, but by not keeping the boys accountable I undermined my words and created a myriad of bad habits. The habit of lying and sneakiness and the habit of laziness. So do what you can do, inspect what you expect, and don't worry too much about what is going on in their hearts. Heck, we often don't know what is going on in our own hearts.

. . . the mistakes I made were often the things I thought at the time were good and wise . . .

Did it really matter that I agonized over a Latin curriculum every single year with only minimal success? Hardly matters at all. But did it matter that my children were reading and being read to? Yes. This was what bore fruit. So many things I worried about at the time don't matter now.

But getting up each day and faithfully carrying out a routine did matter. Morning Time mattered. Going outside mattered. Playing mattered. Smiling mattered. Ice cream mattered. Baseball mattered. My children mattered. But guess what? I mattered too. I am not a huge fan of self-care, but the ultimate thing you can do for yourself is look at Jesus.

❧

Here is a saying that is too true:
A mother is only as happy as her saddest child.

In his masterpiece of sorrow *Silence*, Shusaku Endo writes:

> We priests are in some ways a sad group of men.
> Born into the world to render service to mankind,
> there is no one more wretchedly alone than the
> priest who does not measure up to his task.[8]

I think of this differently. My take is: there is no one more wretchedly alone than a mother who does not measure up to her task.

Thankfully, God has sent me mentors who share their experiences and help me see a way out of this pit of sadness.

Frederick Buechner says:

> As the children started leaving home for lives of
> their own, they left their empty rooms behind so
> that emptiness is another of the things the house
> became full of, beds rarely slept in any more,
> closet doors rarely opened. Any fool knows
> that when you have children, your whole life
> changes, but I was a fool who never realized the
> extent to which when you have your children no
> longer, your life changes again and almost more
> radically . . .
>
> . . . Thinking it over since, I have come to
> believe that maybe another rule came to an end
> along with it. This one was a rule that I had no
> less devastatingly laid down for myself, and it
> was this: that I had no right to be happy unless
> the people I loved—especially my children—

were happy too. I have come to believe that that is not true. I believe instead that we all of us have not only the right to be happy no matter what but also a kind of sacred commission to be happy—in the sense of being free to breathe and move, in the sense of being able to bless our own lives, even the sad times of our own lives, because through all our times we can learn and grow, and through all our times, if we keep our ears open, God speaks to us His saving word.[9]

I loved raising my children, and I love spending time with them now. I love my grandchildren. But more than all of that put together, I love the Lord Jesus Christ. He has fully paid the price for all my sins. Sins so grievous I should definitely be canceled. Not little pretend sins. Real ones.

"For all have sinned and fall short of the glory of God" (Romans 3:23). No matter how hard you try, you can't swim to Hawaii. You are gonna need a life boat, and there is one waiting for you.

A Woman I Know: Donna-Jean Breckenridge

No one wants to be the "Woman I Know" in this category. My good friend Donna-Jean Breckenridge has faced so many hardships, I often marvel that she is still standing. A few years ago she and her husband moved into a multi-generational home with Donna-Jean's parents as well as their daughter and her family. The three men in that family, Donna-Jean's husband, her son-in-law Nate Abrams, and her father, have all passed away since they moved to their home. If you ever read the play *The Trojan Women,* you can just get a picture of what those Breckenridge women have gone through. They are *The Trojan Women* weeping for their lost men. But if you talk to Donna-Jean, you will not be weighed down by her grief. You will be especially buoyed by her trust. She is famous for saying, "God is safe to trust." This is not exactly a popular message these days. Donna-Jean is not pretending that all is well when it clearly is not. She is not pasting on a cardboard smile because "the show must go on." She is weeping. But she is weeping with hope. "If only for this life we have hope in Christ, we are of all people most to be pitied."[10] Donna-Jean has walked with the Lord since she was a small child. Her first memory was hearing her father preach. Her father was her pastor her entire life until he got sick and then died.

> She is weeping. But she is weeping with hope.

Donna-Jean reminds me a little of that other woman of suffering, Elisabeth Elliot, who lost two husbands during her life, and yet is a voice of trust for us, and a woman who reminded us that we are not fools to put our trust in God. Suffering is spiritually discerned.

> The natural person does not accept the things of the Spirit of God, for they are folly to him, and he is not able to understand them because they are spiritually discerned. (1 Corinthians 2:14)

When we trust in God completely, there is a good chance we will face persecution or at least frustration from others.

The Ideal and the Reality

Consider the poem "Up-Hill" from Christina Rossetti:

Up-Hill

Does the road wind up-hill all the way?
Yes, to the very end.
Will the day's journey take the whole long day?
From morn to night, my friend.

But is there for the night a resting-place?
A roof for when the slow dark hours begin.
May not the darkness hide it from my face?
You cannot miss that inn.

Shall I meet other wayfarers at night?
Those who have gone before.
Then must I knock, or call when just in sight?
They will not keep you standing at that door.

Shall I find comfort, travel-sore and weak?
Of labour you shall find the sum.
Will there be beds for me and all who seek?
Yea, beds for all who come.

The first two lines of that poem resonate so much I often find myself quoting them throughout the day.

If we think it is some strange thing that our days are hard, we are going to be tempted to look for solutions and answers. We might even find ourselves googling things we should be praying about, looking to the hive mind rather than the Holy Spirit.

Worse still, if we think it odd that the road is uphill, we might be tempted to quit. We might be tempted to believe that road over there, in the distance with people waving us to join them, is a more even, steady road. There is a story about a couple of guys who thought that. These pilgrims' names were Christian and Faithful, and the easy way led them off the main path where they ended up at Doubting Castle run by Giant Despair and his wife Diffidence (go ahead and look up that word). If you want help finding a way off the hard path and onto the easy way, I am pretty sure you can find a TikTok video that can show you the way.

If we have money, we might be tempted to throw money at the road to smooth the way, and if we are poor, we might be tempted to grow bitter that we cannot escape the uphill way.

Yes, my friends the road winds uphill all the way. Do not think it some strange thing that has happened to you.

Perhaps you may find it comforting today to know that the road winds uphill all the way, as I do. I don't have to fight it or fix it.

I can accept it.

Accepting that the road goes uphill means a couple of things to me.

First, I can slow down. I must slow down. I always tell my family I can handle any hike we take as long as I can go at my own pace. The minute I have to keep up, I become overwhelmed and exhausted. I have learned to be okay with bringing up the rear, even when I lose sight of those ahead of me. It isn't so bad walking quietly alone in the woods. In fact, I have learned to revel in it.

Second, I can rest more. The road is hard, and it requires rest. It doesn't require mani-pedis and spa days, it requires quietness and confidence. I am going to make it to the very end. I know this because the Bible says that He who began a good work in me will complete it. Someday the road will end.

It recently ended for my friend Lynn Bruce. She completed the course; she kept the faith. To the VERY END she kept the faith.

The road goes uphill all the way, but when we reach the end the door shall be opened, and we shall see Him face to face.

"Well done thou good and faithful servant."

Lynn has heard those words.

Let us follow along behind looking to the hills as a place our help comes from, not as a place to fight or fix.

Suggested Reading

Learning to Dance by Michael Mayne

Walking with God through Pain and Suffering by Timothy Keller

The Crook in the Lot by Thomas Boston

In This House of Brede by Rumer Godden

From Fear to Freedom by Rose Marie Miller

Come Back, Barbara by C. John Miller

God's Grace in Your Suffering by David A. Powlinson

Suffering is Never for Nothing by Elisabeth Elliot

The Path of Loneliness by Elisabeth Elliot

The Hiding Place by Corrie Ten Boom

Edges of His Ways by Amy Carmichael

Dark Clouds, Deep Mercy, Discovering the Grace of Lament by Mark Vroegop

Growth Ideas

- Ask for prayer from friends and your church.
- Accept help from others.
- Be gentle with awkward attempts to help.

CHAPTER TEN

The Wise Mother

The fear of the LORD is the beginning of Wisdom.

Proverbs 9:10a

The aged women likewise, that they be in behaviour
as becometh holiness, not false accusers, not given
to much wine, teachers of good things; that they
may teach the young women to be sober, to love
their husbands, to love their children, to be discreet,
chaste, keepers at home, good, obedient to their own
husbands, that the word of God be not blasphemed.

Titus 2:3-5 (KJV)

Katy, bar the door, that is a passage! As a young woman I wanted
to know how to live my life well. I was very critical of the older women. Where the heck were they? Why wouldn't they speak
up? When I was young I could not find them, and I did not know
why. Now that I am older, I know where they are and why they
are so darn hard to find. You see, most older women have made a
lot of mistakes. Like me, my life is riddled with mistakes. Some of
my mistakes have been funny, some of them have been unfortu-
nate, and some have even been devastating. When I talk to young
women, I bring with me a little voice that says, who are you to
be telling them anything? Indeed. Who am I? Older women have
something to share, not in spite of making mistakes, but because

of them. But it is very, very hard to speak up and say, "Here is what I did wrong." Not just because we are ashamed, but also because it is an unpopular message.

Most women, in a utilitarian age, really don't want to hear that. They want to know how to go out there and kick some butt. But the older women often share from broken places. In a world of Elon Musk, Tim Ferriss, canned gratitude, perfect minimalistic contours, and neutral colors without spot or wrinkle, no one wants to know about your mess. The only things we know about failure we learn from memes. One of my favorite lines from TV comes from the show *Madam Secretary*. The secretary and her handsome husband have three children, and they are struggling with their oldest daughter while also trying to avert a crisis in the government. They don't succeed at either task. In response to this, she turns to her husband and says, "Write this on my tombstone: 'She tried hard, but people still got hurt.'"

> Older women have something to share, not in spite of making mistakes, but because of them.

Write that on mine too. Write that on almost every single older mother's headstone. If we want to hear from older women, we are going to have to accept that they are not perfect. Much of our good advice comes in the form of what to avoid, but we also stumbled upon how to do some things right along the way too. It is good to hear the stories of experience from those who have walked the road ahead of us.

Nowadays I disagree with my younger self quite a bit! I recently realized that the internet has been around for more than twenty years. That would be fine, but there are archives of what I said on different forums from twenty years ago. The last twenty years have been a sharp learning curve for me. It is painful to think that I could go back in time and read some of those silly, silly words. Twenty years ago, I was just starting to walk through puberty with my oldest. Today, I have walked through it nine times. I have walked through puberty nine times and menopause once. I would like to see Chuck Norris try that!

Some of the most helpful things older women have said to me have been about their failures. It is comforting to know that you aren't the first person to face a devastating setback.

I once met a joyful older lady who, with her husband, was living with her sister. They had once been jetsetters spanning the globe on yachts and vacations, and then they lost everything and had to move in with her sister. She told me all this with joy on her face and freedom in her heart. I never forgot it.

I have noticed in reading biographies that no one who goes from victory to victory ever gets a biography written about them. Biographies are written about overcomers.

One of the biggest mistakes I made as a homeschool mom was thinking that it was all up to me. As if by bringing human beings into the world, I was now responsible for the rest of their lives, their happiness, their ACT scores, their success—everything was on me. I imagined both my control and my love to be more powerful than they were. With nine children, somebody is always up and someone always down. Sometimes way up *and* way down.

I was carrying these ups and downs through my life as a massive burden. Whether it was the weird moles and the likelihood of melanoma, or the consequences of bad behavior, or just the ups and downs of real life—I carried it. I felt that each twinge my children went through was on me. I partly blame this on the homeschool culture. Homeschooling is good; I believe in it more firmly everyday, or at least some forms of it, but our children are not Frankenstein's monsters. We are not fitting them out with arms and legs and personalities. We need to be careful that we don't imagine ourselves to be more important than we are or our mistakes to be more powerful than they are. Offering ourselves grace is a powerful way to begin to understand how to offer it to others. If you can't forgive yourself, then maybe you don't really understand the unbelievable power of the Gospel.

Titus 2 calls on women to interact with one another over the differing seasons of our lives. Seasons. Summer, winter, spring, and autumn. Days and months grouped together, which we often use as a metaphor for the days of our lives. Women and mothers are uniquely tuned into these seasons. We smell the spring pushing its way up through the frozen winter long before others do. We notice the chill in August before the temperature really changes. We know what lies ahead—The Great Clothing Switch!

As women, maybe at first, these groups of days come neatly one at a time. Later, as we get better at navigating our way through them, they begin to tumble upon us one after the other, taking advantage of our wisdom. When we are young, it is hard to let go of the past season and embrace the new one. We try to live in both seasons. We quickly realize that to live graciously often means saying goodbye to one season so that we can enjoy the new one.

For young moms it may mean saying goodbye to sleeping through the night and hello to embracing the wee midnight hours with a newborn. This calls for change. We might have to give up late date nights with our husband, or fun outings with our friends, or even working on creative projects. For a season. By the time I had my last few babies, those starry, midnight feedings were my favorites. In the daytime, I was competing with so many others for a chance to hold the baby, but in the wee hours of the night, we could look into each others' eyes without interruption, baby and I. Even now, after all these years, that is a bond that cannot be broken.

> We cannot wallow in the past and remain healthy, happy women.

Sometimes these seasonal changes are easy, like when we leave the nest to start our own lives and marriages. How fun is that? We are eager to leave our parents' home and make our own. On the other hand, it is a bit harder on our mother to let us go and embrace her new season of peace and quiet. I used to think the idea of an empty nest syndrome was absurd. Young people are supposed to leave the nest, right? But to the mama who has spent the greater part of her life's energy creating a beautiful nest, mourning its emptiness is not absurd at all. Still, we are older and wiser now. We know that we have to brush ourselves off and take joy in this new season God has called us to. We cannot wallow in the past and remain healthy, happy women. The good news is that this new season often includes grandchildren.

Or what about those seasons that rush in on one another? Have you ever been to a wedding where the bride's or groom's mother was pregnant? How awkward was that? Awkward, but somehow beautiful too. Many women my own age face caring for their youngest teenagers still at home and their aging parents. This can create guilt. When we are doing right by our parents, we feel guilty about neglecting our children, and when we are home taking care of our children, we feel we should be checking in on our parents. This takes wisdom.

Right this minute, each of us is in one season or another, and some of us are finding ourselves in two. Guess what? We are almost always newbies to whatever season we find ourselves in. In life, we are always rookies. Just about the time you get the hang of one season, like being a first-time parent, baby two comes along. Having two children is nothing at all like having one child. Hopefully, you have picked up a little wisdom along the way or at least you have stopped making everyone use hand sanitizer.

Because each of us is always in a new stage of life, two principles should guide how we live. First, we should be gracious to those around us, knowing that they are facing new things in their stage of life as well. I might have had nine children and been a whiz at getting a baby to sleep, but I have never been sixty before and often find it confusing and daunting, just as daunting as those wee hours of the morning thirty-eight years ago when I sat up nursing my first child and crying because I was so very, very tired. By baby two, I was getting plenty of sleep because all I had to do was flip the baby over to the other side. These days sleep is not quite so easy as that. I wake up unexpectedly at 3:00 a.m. and fret over how I am going to make it through the next day. Somehow I always make it, and in the meantime, I am learning. Learning that while I have no baby to gaze at anymore, I do have a heavenly Father to gaze at and thank. Is He not more precious than ten sons?

Second, we should learn from those who have gone before us, even if they walked a slightly different path than we did. They picked up things along the way which we will need. When we reject the generations ahead of us, we are dooming ourselves to mistakes we need not make. I made a lot of mistakes in life which I could have avoided by listening more to older people.

I don't know what season of life you find yourself in, but I am pretty sure you find it challenging. Elizabeth Elliot used to remind me in her writings to "do the next thing." She has left us now, but I look back to you and say it too. "Do the next thing." That turned out to be pretty solid advice.

Do the next thing, and be kind to the mama next to you, especially your own. She is probably having a tough time navigating her season too.

Contentment

Joy brings with it something else entirely.

Contentment.

If we are feeling discontent, it is a trigger that all is not well with our theology. We get frustrated easily. We compare ourselves with others. We grumble and complain. We spend our days trying to fill our hearts with things that can never satisfy.

The opposite of contentment is discontentment. Discontentment is a wily monster popping up almost constantly. You can hardly expect it to be otherwise in a materialistic, utilitarian, social media-driven culture.

We are all given a certain set of circumstances in life. A certain set of parents, a certain socioeconomic standing, certain gifts and talents. That is our lot in life. And it is our job as Christians to find contentment in our lot. Of course, we are allowed to improve ourselves and our lot, but the remedy does not begin with being discontent. If we are discontent, it means we are not paying attention to the little gifts and blessings God is constantly bestowing on us.

The moonrise or the apple blossoms.

The baby that is crying in the next room. Alive and healthy. The very baby you prayed for.

So many, many gifts from God go unnoticed and unappreciated while we scroll through social media wishing we had those dishes or that dress and, for sure, THAT BODY!

Discontentment infects our family. It is like those houses with mold in the Old Testament, where the priest had to keep coming back to see if it was spreading, and finally the house had to be torn down and burned. "For godliness with contentment is great gain. For we brought nothing into this world, and it is certain we can carry nothing out."[1]

There it is, so simply put. Everything is a gift. Learn to be content with what you have, and you will have found great gain. You will then have everything you need for life and godliness. You can then ask your Father for the things you want and wait like a child at Christmas for His gifts. He is fully capable of supplying all your needs.

In my own life, I was always frustrated (that word we like to use instead of angry in our family)—I was always frustrated that I could not afford the curriculum and opportunities other homeschoolers had. I could not see that my children had what they really needed, and what they had was a huge blessing. Instead, I felt jealous and envious of people who could afford to send their children to expensive co-ops and fun groups or buy fancy curricula. If you cannot afford to go to something, that means God has something just as wonderful for your children elsewhere. When we give our attention to God through prayer, we learn to trust Him more and more and more.

I know now that I didn't need all the opportunities I was so angry about that my children were missing. Maybe you can learn from my mistakes. What is frustrating you? The peeling paint? The dirty carpet? You brought nothing into this world. You have shampoo, right? Toothpaste? A library of books? You are good to go.

> . . . open the door, take a deep breath, look around, and see just what great gifts you have been ignoring...

Next time you are discontent, open the door, take a deep breath, look around, and see just what great gifts you have been ignoring while you were lusting after all those false images scrolling by on your phone.

The truth is, contentment is a wonderful feeling while discontentment is miserable. It is completely up to you which one you choose.

The Working Mother

There is another area we need to find contentment and acceptance. That is in our differing choices in regards to work and home. Dorothy Sayers writes:

> We are much too much inclined in these days to divide people into permanent categories, forgetting that a category only exists for its special

231

purpose and must be forgotten as soon as that purpose is served.[2]

As mothers, we know that we all work 24/7, whether we are in the home alone, or working from home to bring in some income, or working outside the home to help our husbands or provide for ourselves. As mothers, we are on call every single hour of every single day. Taking a shower or going to the bathroom are not private moments for moms in some seasons. And certainly there is no expectation of eight hours of sleep at night. Even as an older woman, I am awakened at night to pray for my family. While their cries are no longer pressing, their needs still are.

Then there is the guilt that comes with being responsible for other people. Often when we help one set of people, we are neglecting another set. I found this to happen in everything from changing diapers to baseball. To tell the truth, often no matter how many ball games you attend, it is the ones you miss that the child remembers. That is true for all mothers. But the momma that works outside of her home has a few more layers of guilt to add to her treasure chest of burdens. She may feel judged by moms at home or in her church. Of course, the mom at home also gets a load of guilt too. She may feel the pressure of her parents and others to use that degree so hard won. All our modern freedom cannot free women from the guilt of too many choices.

And this isn't a fantasy guilt. Modern psychologists have noted that more is required of modern parents than any generation in the history of the world. The expectations are immense. While modern parents do more and more for their children, the children appreciate them less and less.[3]

Dorothy Sayers, in her wonderful lecture "Are Women Human?", reminds us that modern roles have been created out of strange cloth. Women and men used to both work in the home, and the home was a place of income and creativity. When the industrial revolution called men away to factories, everything changed. The home was no longer the place of income, but the children were still in the home. At that point, a new model woman was created for the woman: "The Angel in the House." In some ways, women were handed the spiritual reins for their families, and everyone ended up resenting it.

Dorothy Sayers remarks:

> In reaction against the age-old slogan, "woman is the weaker vessel," or the still more offensive, "woman is a divine creature," we have, I think, allowed ourselves to drive into asserting that "a woman is as good as a man," without always pausing to think what exactly we mean by that. What, I feel, we ought to mean is something so obvious that it is apt to escape attention altogether, viz: not that every woman is, in virtue of her sex, as strong, clever, artistic, level-headed, industrious and so forth as any man that can be mentioned; but, that a woman is just as much an ordinary human being as a man, with the same individual preferences, and with just as much right to tastes and preferences of an individual. What is repugnant to every human being is to be

reckoned always as a member of a class and not
as an individual person.[4]

While meaningful, creative work fled the home and efficient
appliances took over much of the labor of homemaking, women
began to feel bored and restless at home. Put on a pedestal but
never given the opportunity to create. In Victorian times, certain
classes of women did not even have the opportunity to care for
their own children, as nannies became the thing.

In our times, women are no longer encouraged to stay home,
and they are not admired for doing so. They are pressured to contribute financially, and many woman do end up working outside
their homes in order to give the family budget a much-needed
boost. And with modernity has come the increase in single parents,
leaving many moms alone to raise and provide for their children.

What a terrible predicament: stay home and be vilified as a
non-contributing member of society, or go to work and be deemed
a bad mother in some circles.

This is a low point in utilitarian and materialistic philosophy.
We neither understand the purpose of work nor the purpose of the
home. We are only left with mommy wars.

After thirty-three years at home educating my children, I was
offered a job outside of my home. Thankfully for me, this was an
organic slide from home to work doing what I had been doing at
home but now in someone's else's home. And without the dirty
laundry and dishes. To be honest, having dropped out of college
to have children and be at home, I really didn't think I was employable. This is a frequent refrain I hear from women at home.

Will I still be employable after "wasting" all those years at home? I thought I would probably go get a job at Chick-fil-A. But it turned out that God had a job waiting for me. I did that job joyfully and meaningfully for four years and then came home and began to work out of my home. I have been astounded that God could use the tools I had gained over the years. This organic transition is perhaps a bit ideal, but it is an ideal to watch for.

But while my time at home reading and reading and reading and thinking and thinking and thinking had prepared me for my new career, it didn't mean that while I was at home I was a "professional" mom. In fact, this is a term that annoys me because it is based on our societal values which give money and income the highest sign of worth. To call a mom at home a "professional" is not to give her credit where credit is due but rather to demean her work, which is priceless.

But no matter whether we work outside the home and then return home or whether we stay at home all the time, our work in the home is priceless.

We may be professionals in our field at work, and there may be some satisfaction in the concrete nature of our worth at work, but when we come home, we all toil in an unappreciated section of society. To put a price tag on this work is a further way to demean it.

You have seen those charts in which what a woman does is reduced to a series of jobs like chauffeur, cook, cleaner, tutor, nanny, etc. After adding up all the salaries, a mother's value is figured at some ridiculously high amount. I get it. This is supposed to make us feel better, but in fact, what it really does is take something that is invaluable and try to make it worth something monetarily because that is the only value moderns seem to understand. Monetary worth is a devaluation of the role of women.

Many working moms long to be at home with their children. Finding contentment when life is not what we hope is hard. Hard, but not impossible. In fact, our very mental health depends upon our accepting the things we cannot change.

Silence and Prayer

Although I have titled this section "Silence and Prayer," the two are often very different things. Maybe opposites. Prayer is talking to God while silence seems to be God talking to us. We can't hear God in all the noise and bustle. It must please our enemy very much that we are distracted by notifications on our devices.

> Our very mental health depends upon our accepting the things we cannot change.

There is nothing passive about prayer. We have to fight to make time for it, and we have to wrestle while we participate in it. When I pray, I am wrestling with God for His will in this world. I am fighting for the defeat of evil and the triumph of good. I am fighting for the souls of my family. I am girding my loins and doing battle.

It is much easier to watch television. Anything will do. Random HGTV shows are especially helpful here. I once, and only once, watched a show about someone named Honey-Boo-Boo for thirty whole minutes. You can't tell me that was not a distraction from prayer. The magnitude of what I was doing should have alerted me to the fact that a battle needed to be waged. The most encouraging thing about prayer is the answers. It always seems to me that when

God allows us to pray for something, it is because it is a work He is completing, and He is allowing us to be a part of that work.

A few years ago, I woke up at 4:30 in the morning and could not go back to sleep. This drove me batty for an hour, when it finally occurred to me that perhaps I was awake for a reason. Perhaps I needed to be praying for someone. It was a Thursday morning, and I had visited my father in skilled care on the Sunday before. He was laboring to breathe and to talk, and it was agonizing to watch. For the first time in all these many months if felt like too much. In those wee hours of that Thursday morning, I started to pray for my dad. I started to pray that God would release him. That he would not have to suffer anymore. That he would go to sleep and wake up in heaven. I looked at my phone, and it was 5:36 a.m. At 5:40 a.m. my father stopped breathing forever. At 5:40 a.m. my father woke up in heaven.

God had awakened me to participate in this moment in time, and all I could think about was getting enough sleep. But God was kind and eventually my mind did turn to prayer, which is probably why I was awakened at 4:30 a.m. and not 5:30 a.m. My prayers didn't affect God's workings so much as God allowed me to be a part of what He was doing. Through prayer, God allowed me to participate in my father's death, even though I could not be there physically as I longed to be. That is my view on prayer.

When the Holy Spirit reminds us to pray, we can be sure that God is at work. Prayer, then, is not so much begging God for shiny baubles as it is asking to be a part of the work God is doing. In that way, prayer itself becomes the encouragement to pray. When I pray, my eyes are wide awake to God's workings in the world. It is the ultimate way of seeing. If, as I have proposed throughout this book, education is a way of seeing, then prayer is the greatest educational tool we have available. When we see Him, we shall be like Him.

In the novel *Kristin Lavransdatter*, Kristin is the mother of seven sons. You could say that she has varying results with her boys. She loves them each very much, but in the third and final section of the book she removes herself from their daily lives to spend time in a monastery praying. When I was young and read this, it seemed like a defeat. She has given up on her family. But now that I am older, I completely understand her choice. She has done everything she could for her family, and now she must do the last and most important task. She must pray. That is the ultimate job of the grandmother. We look up and see a tidal wave of things outside of our control, and we can either panic or pray. But we can do more than pray. We can pray and trust. We don't have to panic. God is bigger than all your hopes and dreams for your family. His business is redemption. Praying is how we get to be a part of the family business. Praying doesn't always feel hopeful, especially in the wee hours of the morning when anxiety can wrack us. But praying is the path to peace. It is the single most important thing we will do with our lives.

Our modern utilitarianism has blinded us to the ministry of prayer. Housebound, sick, or elderly Christians may do more for the kingdom of God than we ever realize. If we find our nest empty and time heavy on our hands, it is time to learn to pray. Sometimes on Thursday mornings, I sneak away from my house and attend the prayer meeting at our church. The thing I love most about that meeting is that it is filled with elderly men and women. I like to keep an eye on the people in the season of life ahead of me. The second thing I love is their prayers. They are never anguished. They are just ordinary requests to their Father, as if they have every reason to believe that He hears them. It amazes me every single time.

God is at work. We pray. We see the hand of God at work.

☙

Silence is something else altogether. Once we have prayed, we should be alert for answers to our prayers. Sometimes we are not alert, but often the Holy Spirit reminds us to be alert. I have found moments of silence greatly aid in my awareness of God's voice which is described in the Bible as a still, small voice. When silence rushes into my life accidentally, it is such a glaring contrast I am forced to heed it. Last night, I was at a little party in my neighborhood. As I left the party, I walked out into the silent, dark street. Often when we stand in the dark, the glow from homes is alluring, inviting. But sometimes when we have left the glow, the darkness and silence has its own allure. We walk out of the artificial light of a home to the softer gleam of the night sky. The breeze touches our cheek, and we are suddenly alone in the universe. Alone, but not alone. The thoughts we have pushed asunder and shielded ourselves from creep forward. Maybe. But sometimes they are kept at bay by bigger things. The moon. The breeze. The glory of God. We are small in the universe, and that is comforting. There are more things in heaven and earth than are dreamt of in our philosophy, our theology. Something, someone else is entirely in control of the world, and that is someone we can trust. We can let go of those scary thoughts, and those sad ones, and we can know. In the silence, we can know. We can hear too. We can hear the voice of the turtle dove in the land. We hear the voice of the turtle dove, and we know as we are known. Silence. We don't love it. Sometimes it burns. Burning off the dross of our lesser selves. But when we learn to love it, we are on our way to knowing as we are known.

Someday we will truly be educated.

> Beloved, we are God's children now, and what we will be has not yet appeared; but we know that when he appears we shall be like him, because we shall see him as he is. (1 John 3:2)

There it is again. The truth about education. First we see, then we know.

Or again, 1 Corinthians 13:11-12:

> When I was a child, I spoke like a child, I thought like a child, I reasoned like a child. When I became a man, I gave up childish ways. For now we see in a mirror dimly, but then face to face. Now I know in part; then I shall know fully, even as I have been fully known.

God fully knows us now. He is completely educated. He never comes to that place of "I don't know," and when we see Him, gaze at Him, pay attention to Him, we will KNOW. In chapter one, we started with "I don't know," and here we end this book with the final truth. We will know, even as we are known. Doesn't that make you want to take communion right now! The Heidelberg Catechism question one asks and answers:

What is your only comfort in life and in death?

That I am not my own, but belong—body and soul, in life and in death—to my faithful Savior, Jesus Christ. He has fully paid for all my sins with His precious blood, and has set me free from the tyranny of the devil.

He also watches over me in such a way that not a hair can fall from my head without the will of my Father in heaven; in fact, all things must work together for my salvation.

Because I belong to Him, Christ, by His Holy Spirit, assures me of eternal life and makes me wholeheartedly willing and ready from now on to live for Him.

I would be remiss if I did not acknowledge that as women we are under assault night and day with images and imaginations of self-help and betterment. It is my greatest fear that this book will be a part of the therapeutic nature of modern womanhood. That ideal where we are encouraged to look within to find ourselves. That the ultimate truth is within. It is utterly exhausting to search for something that cannot and will not ever be found. The platitudes and memes are exhausting. I hope this book is not just one more voice telling you that you can change and be a better you. The Heidelberg Catechism question 1 is so excellently put together that it is almost a weapon in itself against this dreadful disease that plagues us.

What is my only hope? That I am not my own!! I belong to someone else. It just happens to be the God of the universe. This is such an amazing truth. It frees me from so many false ideas. I am not my own!!

Many of you may remember my joy in finding out that I was not the potter shaping the clay of my children. This is equally as wonderful as that moment was for me.

I am not my own!!

This point was really brought home to me this year while reading Alan Noble's book titled *You Are Not Your Own*. I had read and read and read about the nature of modern therapeutic culture, a culture that I could clearly see was negative and deadly, but it took Alan's book to remind me of the most glorious truth that I am not my own. This really is the final solution to what ails modernity. We have thrown off the old gods and replaced them with ourselves.

> If you are your own and belong to Christ, then your personhood is a real creation, objectively sustained by God. And as a creation of God, you have no obligation to create your self. Your identity is based on God's perfect will, not your own subjective, uncertain will. All your efforts to craft a perfect, marketable image add nothing to your personhood. The reason the opinions of others don't define you isn't because your opinion is the only one that counts, but because you are not reducible to any human efforts of definition. The only being who can fully know you and understand you without reducing you to a stereotype or an idol is God.[5]

A Woman I Know: You

Since writing my first book *Mere Motherhood*, I have met many of you. I am always amazed at how sweet you are about the book. Most of you say that you feel like we are friends, and you know me well. This makes me smile. I don't know each of you as individuals, but I do think I know your heart, your desires, what you want for your children and your families, how you want to live your lives, and how hard it is to live up to those high ideals. We are not so very different at all. We have different talents and successes, but we all carry around the fear that we are not enough. Why wouldn't we?

My son recently expressed concern that by writing and speaking I gave people the impression we had a perfect family. This made me smile because the more I tell you how broken and sad parts of our family were and are, the more you come to me to tell me your stories. It seems that most of you have already learned that relationships are hard and communication faulty. You want to know that there is life after failure and disappointment. And that is what I do know.

Here is a line I really love from a song: "As you speak a hundred billion failures disappear," and then, "You're the One who never leaves the one behind."[6]

You have been bought with a price.

It all matters.

The Ideal and the Reality

Here we are at the end. The final reality check. We have talked about the ideal over and over again. We have checked it against the somewhat disappointing reality of our days. Who among us has it all? Which of you is the composite woman? The Thinking Mother who spends her leisure learning, the Contemplative Mother who never neglects her appointments with God, the Reading Mother who uses her seconds to store up treasures in her heart, the Natural Mother who never misses a chance to take a nature hike, the Active Mother on her way to the gym even now, the Studious Mother studying deeply and not just broadly, the Creative Mother filling her lovely home with her handiwork, the Beautiful Mother cherished and noticed by everyone, the Suffering Mother weeping for her children, and the Wise Mother who knows she can't have it all—not even all of these good things.

. . . while you cannot have it all, you can have ever so much more than you ever imagined.

Since we cannot have it all, must we choose therefore nothing? I hope this book has encouraged you to understand that while you cannot have it all, you can have ever so much more than you ever imagined. You can choose to order your days and your leisure. You can cherish the tiny moments that make up our lives. You can hide God's Word in your heart so that sin is kept at bay, at least some of the time.

We are mamas. We have taken on a project we cannot possibly succeed at by ourselves. We are so out of our league, we hardly know how to judge each day. We have only one hope: the hope that the God who formed a hundred billion galaxies and stars and moons sees us, knows us, and will bless our humble efforts beyond what we could ever ask or imagine.

Lift Up Your Eyes

Now to him who is able to keep you from stumbling and to present you blameless before the presence of his glory with great joy, to the only God, our Savior, through Jesus Christ our Lord, be glory, majesty, dominion, and authority, before all time and now and forever. Amen. (Jude 1:24-25)

Suggested Reading

The White Stone: The Art of Letting Go by Esther de Waal

Let Evening Come by Jane Kenyon

You Are Not Your Own by Alan Noble

The Rise and Triumph of the Modern Self by Carl Trueman

Suggested Course of Study

Start your own Morning Time.

Mother's Morning Meeting

- Breathe for two minutes.
- Read Bible.
- Read devotional.
- Listen to a classical music piece.
- Do a puzzle (Sudoku, crossword, or logic).
- Stretch.
- Read several books slowly over time.
- Do this outside whenever possible.

Endnotes

Chapter 1: The Thinking Mother

1. Marcus Tullius Cicero, *Cicero on the Ideal Orator (De Oratore)* (New York: Oxford University Press, 2001).

2. David V. Hicks, *Norms & Nobility: A treatise on education* (Lanham, MD: University Press of America, 1999), 78.

3. James Madison, *The Papers of James Madison,* edited by William T. Hutchinson et al. (Chicago and London: University of Chicago Press, 1962–77 vols. 1–10; Charlottesville: University Press of Virginia, 1977–vols. 11–), https://press-pubs.uchicago.edu/founders/documents/v1ch16s23.html.

4. David V. Hicks, *Norms & Nobility: A treatise on education* (Lanham, MD: University Press of America, 1999), 80.

5. Hicks, *Norms & Nobility,* 80.

6. Hicks, *Norms & Nobility,* 80.

7. Hicks, *Norms & Nobility,* 81.

8. "The end then of Learning is to repair the ruins of our first parents by regaining to know God aright, and out of that knowledge to love him, to imitate him, to be like him, as we may the nearest by possessing our souls of true virtue, which being united to the heavenly grace of faith makes up the highest perfection." John Milton, *Of Education* (1664). Accessed November 2023, https://milton.host.dartmouth.edu/reading_room/of_education/text.shtml.

9. Although this line doesn't appear in his written work, it is commonly attributed to Churchill and captures his determined spirit.

10. Christopher Klein, "Winston Churchill's World War Disaster," History.com, accessed November 2023, https://www.history.com/news/winston-churchills-world-war-disaster.

Chapter 2: The Contemplative Mother

1. Canadian founder of the Christian Missionary and Alliance church.

2. "I am Loved," a song by Gloria and William J. Gaither, 1978.

3. The ESV Daily Bible Reading Plan and the M'Cheyne One Year Plan are

both available as PDFs from https://www.esv.org/resources/reading-plans/ as of this writing.

4. Peter Scazzero, *Emotionally Healthy Spirituality Day by Day: A 40-Day Journey with the Daily Office* (Grand Rapids, MI: Zondervan, 2008, 2014, 2018), 12.

5. Stratford Caldecott, *Beauty in the Word: Rethinking the Foundations of Education* (Tacoma, WA: Angelico Press, 2012), 30-31, Kindle.

6. Phyllis Tickle, *The Divine Hours,* 3 vols (New York: Doubleday, 2000-2001).

7. "When people insist on perfection or nothing they get nothing," Edith Schaeffer, *What is a Family?* (Grand Rapids, MI: Baker Books, 1975, reprinted 1997), 74.

8. John Cowart, *Strangers on the Earth* (Jacksonville, FL: Bluefish Books, 2006), 97.

9. Romans 8:1

Chapter 3: The Reading Mother

1. "Hot Reading Challenge Tips from Pros Who Read More Than 100 Books a Year," Goodreads.com (blog), accesssed November 27, 2023, https://www.goodreads.com/blog/show/1294-hot-reading-challenge-tips-from-pros-who-read-more-than-100-books-a-year.

2. C. S. Lewis, *The Four Loves* (New York: Harcourt Brace Modern Classic, 1960, reprinted 1991), 65.

3. Dorothy Sayers, *Strong Poison* (New York: Harper Paperbacks, 1930, reprinted 1995), 132.

4. G. K. Chesterton, "Our Notebook," *The Illustrated London News,* July 5, 1924, 6.

5. From their website: "AmblesideOnline is a free homeschool curriculum that uses Charlotte Mason's classically-based principles to prepare children for a life of rich relationships with everything around them: God, humanity, and the natural world." https://www.amblesideonline.org/

6. The Great Books of the Western World was a book series published by Encyclopedia Brittanica in 1952. The term "Great Books" refers to this set of classics, but also refers more broadly to books that are recognized to be part of the "the great conversation of ideas," a term coined by Robert Maynard Hutchins for the book set.

7. Visit https://houseofhumaneletters.com/to learn more about these classes. Discover *The Literary Life Podcast* at https://www.theliterary.life/ or wherever you like to listen to podcasts.

8. C. S. Lewis, introduction to *On the Incarnation: The Treatise De Incarnatione Verbi Dei* by Saint Athanasius, trans. and ed. A Religious of C. S. M. V. (Crestwood, NY: St Vladimir's Seminary Press, 1998), 4.

9. Erasmus's words in a letter to James Batt ("Epistle 113") were, "I have been applying my whole mind to the study of Greek; and as soon as I receive any money I shall first buy Greek authors, and afterwards some clothes." This is popularly restated as "When I have a little money I buy books; and if I have any left, I buy food and clothes." Refer to *The Epistles of Erasmus from His Earliest Letters to His Fifty-First Year Arranged in Order of Time*, Trans. by Francis Morgan Nichols (London: Longmans, Green, and Co., 1901), 236.

Chapter 4: The Natural Mother

1. Charlotte Mason, *Home Education*, vol. 1 of *The Home Education Series* (London: Kegan Paul, Trench, Trubner, & Co., Ltd, 1906), 61.

2. J. R. R. Tolkien, *The Fellowship of the Ring*, 2nd ed. (Boston: Houghton Mifflin Company), 83.

3. Tristan Gooley, *The Lost Art of Reading Nature's Signs: Use Outdoor Clues to Find Your Way, Predict the Weather, Locate Water, Track Animals—and Other Forgotten Skills*, (New York: The Experiment Publishing, 2015), 7.

4. Thomas Merton, "Rain and the Rhinoceros," in *Raids on the Unspeakable* (New York: New Directions Publishing, 1966), 9-10.

5. Psalm 27:10 (KJV)

6. Charlotte Mason, *Home Education*, vol. 1 of *The Home Education Series* (London: Kegan Paul, Trench, Trubner, & Co., Ltd, 1906), 32.

7. Wikipedia's "Philology" entry, accessed November 27, 2023, https://en.wikipedia.org/wiki/Philology.

Chapter 5: The Active Mother

1. Teresa Tapp is the author of *Fit and Fabulous in 15 Minutes* (New York: Ballantine Books, 2006) and her workouts can be found online at her YouTube channel, https://www.youtube.com/@TTappInc.

2. Psalm 127:2b (NKJV)

3. "But the Lord answered her, 'Martha, Martha, you are anxious and troubled about many things, but one thing is necessary. Mary has chosen the good portion, which will not be taken away from her.'" (Luke 10:41-42)

Chapter 6: The Studious Mother

1. AmblesideOnline Year One booklist, https://www.amblesideonline.org/ao-y1-bks.

2. Khan Academy, https://www.khanacademy.org/.

3. Lewis Carroll coined the word "frabjous," which appears in his poem "Jabberwocky": "'And hast thou slain the Jabberwock? / Come to my arms, my beamish boy! / O frabjous day! Callooh! Callay!' / He chortled in his joy." "Jabberwocky" appeared in Carroll's book *Through the Looking-glass and What*

Alice Found There (New York: MacMillan and Company, 1875), 21.

4. "Vulgar" in this sense means "common."

5. Annie Dillard, *Pilgrim at Tinker Creek* (New York: Harper Perennial Modern Classics, 2007), 10.

6. Mars Hill Audio says this about The Mars Hill Audio Journal: "Our flagship product, the MARS HILL AUDIO Journal, is an 'audio magazine' featuring over two hours of conversation with perceptive and engaging thinkers on each quarterly digital volume. Guests on the Journal examine the ideas, institutions, preoccupations, and fashionable assumptions that shape our cultural lives. They include scholars from a wide range of disciplines, most of whom are authors of recent books investigating some aspect of our cultural experience and the interaction of ideas, practices, and institutions that have created the conditions in which we now live." Accessed December 2023, https://marshillaudio.org/collections/mars-hill-audio-journal.

7. The Open University, https://www.open.edu/openlearn/free-courses/full-catalogue.

Chapter 7: The Creative Mother

1. *The Death of Christian Culture* (Norfolk, VA: IHS Press, 2008), 27, Accessed November 27, 2023, https://christusliberat.org/journal/wp-content/uploads/2017/10/The-Death-of-Christian-Culture-John-Senior.pdf.

2. Luanne Shackelford, "Climbing Mount Never-Rest," chapter 5 in *A Survivor's Guide to Home Schooling* (Wheaton, IL: Crossway, 1988), 27-40.

3. John Hodges, conversation with the author.

4. The Great Courses, https://www.thegreatcourses.com/.

5. Karen Mains, *Open Heart, Open Home,* (Wheaton, IL: Mainstay Church Resources, 1998), 14.

Chapter 8: The Beautiful Mother

1. 1 Samuel 16:7b

2. "Discretion" *The Oxford Pocket Dictionary of Current English*, Encyclopedia.com, accessed November 27, 2023, https://www.encyclopedia.com/humanities/dictionaries-thesauruses-pictures-and-press-releases/discretion-1.

3. C. S. Lewis, *Mere Christianity,* (New York: Harper Collins, 1952, 2001), 131.

4. Rudyard Kipling, "The Female of the Species."

5. Edward Rowland Sill, "The Fool's Prayer," *stanza 6.*

Chapter 9: The Suffering Mother

1. Elisabeth Elliot, *Suffering is Never for Nothing,* (Nashville, TN: B&H Books, 2019), 13, Kindle.

2. Elisabeth Elliot, *Suffering is Never for Nothing*, 35, Kindle.

3. Elisabeth Elliot, *Suffering is Never for Nothing*, 35, Kindle.

4. David A. Powlinson, *God's Grace in Your Suffering*, (Wheaton, IL: Crossway, 2018), 62.

5. Mark Vroegop, *Dark Clouds, Deep Mercy: Discovering the Grace of Lament*, (Wheaton, IL: Crossway, 2019), 26.

6. Vroegop, *Dark Clouds, Deep Mercy*, 26.

7. Jeannette Tulis, conversation with the author.

8. Shusaku Endo, *Silence: A Novel*, (London: Picador Classics, 2016), 18.

9. Frederick Buechner, *Telling Secrets*, (New York: Harper Collins, 1991), 55, 102.

10. 1 Corinthians 15:19 (NIV)

Chapter 10: The Wise Mother

1. 1 Timothy 6:6-7 (NASB)

2. Dorothy Sayers, "Are Women Human? Address given to a Women's Society, 1938," *Are Women Human?* (Grand Rapids, MI: William B. Eerdmans Publishing), 33.

3. Joshua Coleman, "A Shift in American Family Values Is Fueling Estrangement," *The Atlantic*, January 2021, https://www.theatlantic.com/family/archive/2021/01/why-parents-and-kids-get-estranged/617612/.

4. Dorothy Sayers, "Are Women Human? Address given to a Women's Society, 1938," *Are Women Human?* (Grand Rapids, MI: William B. Eerdmans Publishing), 19.

5. Alan Noble, *You Are Not Your Own* (Downers Grove, IL: InterVarsity Press), 139.

6. "So Will I (100 Billion X)," a song by Hillsong UNITED from their album *Wonder*, written by Joel Houston, Benjamin William Hastings & Michael Fatkin, 2018.

About the Author

Cindy Rollins homeschooled her nine children for over thirty years. She is the host of *The New Mason Jar* podcast and a co-host with Angelina Stanford and Thomas Banks of the popular *Literary Life Podcast*. She also curates the "Over the Back Fence Newsletter" at MorningTimeForMoms.com. She is the author of *Mere Motherhood: Morning Time, Nursery Rhymes, and My Journey Toward Sanctification*; *Morning Time: A Liturgy of Love*; *The Literary Life Commonplace Books* and the *Mere Motherhood Newsletters*.

Cindy runs an active Patreon group where the participants read Charlotte Mason's volumes and discuss questions pertaining to motherhood and life. Her heart's desire is to encourage moms using Charlotte Mason's timeless principles. She lives in Chattanooga, Tennessee, with her husband, Tim, and dog, Max. She also travels around the world visiting her many grandchildren and occasionally speaks at events.

Website: morningtimeformoms.com
Facebook: CindyRollinsWriter
Instagram: @cindyordoamoris
Mere Motherhood Facebook Group: MereMotherhood
Patreon: patreon.com/cindyrollins

Cindy's Patreon   MorningTimeForMoms.com

Don't miss these titles by Cindy Rollins

  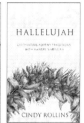

Morning Time: A Liturgy of Love
The Morning Time Student Anthology
Hallelujah: Cultivating Advent Traditions with Handel's Messiah
The Literary Life Commonplace Books
The Literary Life KIDS Commonplace Books

Also From Blue Sky Daisies

More from Blue Sky Daisies

Charlotte Mason
*Charlotte Mason: The Teacher Who Revealed Worlds of Wonder by Lanaya Gore and illlustrated by Twila Farmer
*The Charlotte Mason Book of Quotes: Copywork to Inspire by Lanaya Gore

Geography Books
*Elementary Geography by Charlotte Mason
*Home Geography for Primary Grades with Written and Oral Exercises by C. C. Long

Language Arts and Grammar Books
*The Mother Tongue: Adapted for Modern Students by George Lyman Kittredge
  In this series: Workbook 1 and 2; Answer Key 1 and 2
Exercises in Dictation by F. Peel
*Grammar Land: Grammar in Fun for the Children of Schoolroom Shire (Annotated) by M. L. Nesbitt and annotated by Amy M. Edwards and Christina J. Mugglin

The CopyWorkBook®

The CopyWorkBook: Writings of Charlotte Mason by Lanaya Gore
The CopyWorkBook: George Washington's Rules of Civility & Decent Behavior in Company and Conversation by Amy M. Edwards and Christina J. Mugglin
The CopyWorkBook: Comedies of William Shakespeare by Amy M. Edwards and Christina J. Mugglin

Other Titles
Umbrellas by Twila Farmer
The Birds' Christmas Carol by Kate Douglas Wiggin
The Innkeeper's Daughter by Michelle Lallement
Kipling's Rikki-Tikki-Tavi: A Children's Play by Amy M. Edwards

*These titles are popular with those inspired by Charlotte Mason and her educational philosophy.